MW01091748

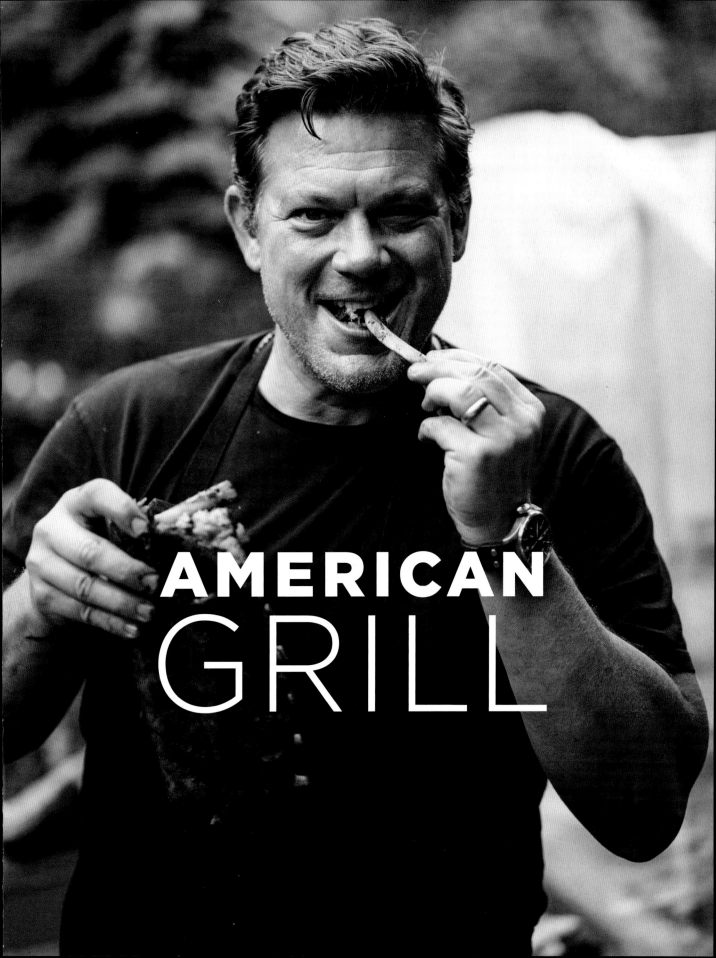

AMERICAN
GRILL

AMERICAN GRILL

A COOKBOOK

125 Recipes for Mastering Live Fire

TYLER FLORENCE

Abrams, New York

CONTENTS

FOREWORD

BY ALICE WATERS

THERE IS NOTHING ELSE LIKE COOKING OVER AN OPEN FIRE. It has practically been written into our DNA since the beginning of civilization: it is the most primal, immediate way to transform food from raw ingredients into something aromatic, hot, flavorful, and delicious. Grilling over a wood fire is my favorite way to cook—it's the place in the kitchen where I feel the most comfortable and at home—because of the way it awakens people's senses. When my daughter was growing up, I would wake up early and make a fire in our kitchen hearth so I could lure her out of bed and downstairs with the aroma of grilled peppers or a fried egg, cooked right in the very heart of the fire. It worked every time—even when she was a teenager, which is saying something.

Through the years, cooking over fire became a hallmark of Chez Panisse. We grilled lobsters in seaweed in the backyard; we built an open hearth in our kitchen and have made everything from grilled leeks to roast chicken to fish soups like bouillabaisse; one time, we even placed a spit right out in our courtyard and cooked a whole wild boar in front of the restaurant for New Year's Eve. The beauty of grilling is that it can allow ingredients to shine on their own, intensifying and heightening their natural flavors—and when you are cooking with ripe, locally grown organic ingredients, it means you need to do very little to make something taste delicious. What could be simpler? The origins of the fuel you are using matter, too, and there are ways to ensure you are making fires sustainably: for example, I buy wood for my fires from environmentally conscious firewood suppliers who are also planting trees at the same time. Plus, chemical additives in certain fuel sources will creep into the taste of your food, whereas different types of woods (oak, fig, grapevine) will infuse meat, poultry, and fish with delightfully different flavors. There is a simplicity and logic to grilling—an easy-to-understand cause and effect—but there is also a wildness and magic to it; when we are tending the coals or watching the flicker of the flames, it is a reminder of our origins, and of our place in nature.

I've always said that the best way to learn how to grill is just through trial and error, touching and testing as you go. Grilling is generous in that way: you can take a fish off, open it up, put it back if it's not quite done; if a rack of lamb is cooking too fast, you can move it to a section of the grill where the fire underneath is mellower. Grilling is a lesson in improvisation, in being present and engaged in the moment—a lesson that I know Tyler deeply understands. This book is a beautiful road map to grilling, born out of Tyler's lifelong love for it. He demystifies the process for first-time grillers, and his recipes open up new avenues for more experienced cooks: you'll find flavors here from all over the world, from smoky babaganoush and grilled pita bread to Korean-style chicken wings to pork chile verde made with charred tomatillos, onions, and poblanos. Most of all, Tyler welcomes you in, so that the process of lighting a fire and cooking over it feels like the most natural thing in the world.

INTRODUCTION

THE ALARM STARTLED ME FROM SLEEP AT 4:30 A.M. ON A COLD JANUARY MORNING. It was dark and damp outside; days of rain had soaked the yard and hills outside my Marin County, California, home. But nothing was going to stop me from getting out of bed.

Today was brisket day.

I pulled the dry-rubbed, twelve-pound slab from the refrigerator, threw on a heavy rain jacket, and went outside to fire up the smoker. By 6:00 A.M., I was cranking. I had rigged a tarp overhead, ignited the chimney, fed the charcoal box, and raked a layer of applewood on top. The brisket was in.

As wisps of scented smoke curled their way into the yard, I had a vision of my father doing something similar one Thanksgiving morning when I was seven. I looked on as he messed with our holiday turkey on this old domed Weber device, dressed in his heavy Air Force field parka as he started a long day of babysitting the smoker.

At just that moment, my wife, Tolan, opened the side door. She looked up at the thunderous sky, looked at the smoker, and looked at me, already dripping, like I was seven different kinds of crazy.

I just smiled. This, right here, was my happy place.

I have always joked with people that I grew up with barbecue sauce in my baby bottle; to this day, the smell of hickory and mesquite brings me instantly back to my childhood in Greenville, South Carolina, where cooking over charcoal and smoked wood wasn't just a pastime but a religion as true as the one that brought us to church on Sundays. I learned the art of good barbecue not just by watching my dad and sampling grilled family recipes at Sunday cookouts, but by tasting and studying the barbecue that defined the Carolinas—one of the four pillars of the great American tradition—up and down my home state.

The comfort and pull of that tradition, of that ceremony—because that's what grilling and smoking

really is—has continued to stick with me as I've grown up and made my own way through three decades in the culinary world and of my adulthood. It's been there, providing inspiration, as I've opened multiple restaurants on both coasts, filmed nearly thirty years of television shows, written seventeen cookbooks, and raised a family in Northern California.

A few years ago, I turned fifty. As one does during big birthdays, I got to reflecting on my life—where I've been, where I plan on going. And I had a bit of an epiphany that in many ways led me here, to this book.

Like many adults my age, I'm exceptionally busy. I run an ever-growing group of restaurants based out of San Francisco, and when I'm not behind the stoves I'm either filming, cooking at special events, going to food festivals, or making other in-person appearances. The truth is, I'm not really in charge of my own schedule. I find out each morning what's on the docket and jump in headfirst. When I finally *do* get home, I want to spend time with my family, to relieve my wife of the logistical stuff she so willingly takes care of while I'm gone, and to get a few moments with her and our kids. And I love every second of that—I feel so incredibly lucky to have the career I do and still go home to the unwaveringly supportive Florence crew.

But it does, in a way, feel like I'm constantly answering to someone else—and I think this is something to which most of my friends and contemporaries can relate. So when I thought about what *I* like to do, what makes *me* happy, I realized that there are very few outlets in my life—two, really—that are just for me.

The first is riding my motorcycle. Give me a sunny day, open road, the wind at my back—few things are more therapeutic for me.

The second is grilling.

I've always felt that there's almost a spiritual feeling to cooking over a live fire. It's meat and heat, time and temperature. It has instructions but it also has room for interpretation. It's primal, but it's also precise. There's a level of stoicism and solitude to grilling that gives us a project, something to do with our hands, and allows us to spend time with friends, if we choose, but more often, alone. That solo time, the scent of wood smoke or charcoal lulling me into a relaxed state, is how I recharge my batteries while continuing to produce something special—also very important for my creative side.

It's what led me here, seventeen cookbooks later. *American Grill* is an anthology of this passion of mine, one I've spent decades cultivating—ignited by my childhood surroundings but stoked by the hours I've spent standing by the grill or smoker, processing my week or sharing a beer with a friend. What has come off the grates during those sessions has found its way into a collection that I hope is as useful and helpful to others as it has been to me, my family, and friends.

And as the name suggests, it represents a portrait of American outdoor cuisine as it is today, which is to say not simply barbecue chicken, ribs, coleslaw, and potato salad—though you'll find some of the best versions of those within these pages—but recipes that are globally influenced, as much of American food now is. Between the dry-rubbed brisket and Buffalo shrimp skewers, you'll find Vietnamese-style pork noodle bowls, pollo asado, grilled green curry mussels, and bulgogi. Mac and cheese will go back to back in the Sides chapter with asparagus draped in miso sesame sauce. And so on.

I've been grateful for the opportunity to put together this collection, which, like each of my other sixteen books, serves as a snapshot of a particular moment in my life.

When I wrote *Dinner at My Place*, for example, my son Hayden had just turned one, and eating meals no longer meant going to the new hot restaurants around the city. Dinner, literally, was now happening at my place. *Start Fresh* chronicles the year I created what became a very successful line of fresh, organic baby food after my daughter, Dorothy, was born—the first of its kind to go in pouches. *Inside the Test Kitchen* and *Tyler's Ultimate* were companion cookbooks to shows I was filming on Food Network during those years.

These time capsules of my life have been an honor to share. When we create a book—and I say we,

because these are always a collective team effort—it allows us to connect with people exactly where we are.

This is where I am now. In the past few years, I've opened my dream restaurant—a modern American steakhouse called Miller & Lux—that allows me to both cook and serve incredible cuts of beef, fresh seafood, and seasonal sides, and educate my diners on the virtues of having a responsibly ranched, sustainably sourced steak on occasion. It comes as no shock to anyone that my brand has become an elevated version of meat and potatoes, chops and creamed kale, fried chicken and truffled mac and cheese. As I said, those early influences have been morphing themselves into what has become my signature style, honed over several decades. And though during work hours that shows itself in a gleaming stainless-steel restaurant kitchen and elegantly designed dining room, it plays out at home over charcoal in the backyard.

My kids are now teenagers and have grown up to the point where I'm lucky if I get a grunt and a nod on their way out the door (unless it's to ask me for a ride to Starbucks), and so I have a little more time to lend to the hobbies I love. For now, that's a few hours—or sometimes even less—raking the coals, flipping the steaks, and of course, smoking that brisket—with the goal that we can all enjoy it together at the end of the day. Because that's still the best part.

I think you'll feel the same. By the time you've cooked your way through *American Grill*, I hope the pages are smudged with barbecue sauce and stained with steak oil. I hope the recipes give you the opportunity to spend a moment giving something to yourself, with an outcome that will both delight and impress your people.

Enjoy the process, share the results. That's what it's all about. Even if, on occasion, that means getting up while it's still dark outside.

YOUR GRILL IS AN OVEN

HOW TO USE THIS BOOK

IT ALL STARTED WITH A SMASH BURGER.

The smash burger is one of my signature recipes, which I developed years ago and have probably made hundreds of times at this point. I will die on the hill that says it rivals In-N-Out, and to know me is to know I like few things more than In-N-Out. It's essential that the burgers be grilled on a cast-iron flattop griddle, not straight on the grill grates. The patties should be whisper thin, which is what makes them cook up so beautifully lacy-crisp and juicy, but it also means that they'd fall right through if they didn't have something stabilizing them underneath. And so on the very first day of shooting photos for this book, out came the griddle.

As we worked our way through the recipes being shot, the cast-iron accessories just kept coming. A large skillet for Mediterranean Cast-Iron Calamari (page 33), a hefty Dutch oven for Pork Chile Verde (page 169) there—even grill-safe baking vessels for desserts. At some point we started joking around that I didn't even need an indoor kitchen, we were doing literally everything on the grill.

But here's the thing. Your grill *is* an oven. *And* a stovetop. It's even a warming drawer when you need to hold something at temp. And it's a microwave when you want to heat up something quickly, or make popcorn. (Don't sleep on the Caramel Kettle Corn, page 225.)

Don't get me wrong. There are still plenty of straight-up grilling recipes in here that get cooked in minutes directly over high heat with those stunning grill marks that make you look like a pro: Kids' Chicken Tender Tacos (page 98), Grilled Shrimp Cocktail (page 29), fragrant Beef Kofta (page 120).

You'll also notice that many recipes in the book start out by instructing you to set up your grill for both direct *and* indirect cooking, with a hot side and cold side. This allows you to control multiple zones on your grill without charring the living daylights out of whatever goes straight on the grates, on top of a blistering-hot fire. It achieves that oven effect I'm talking about, with more circular, ambient heat. And it will open up your outdoor cooking world in ways you never thought possible.

I love cooking this way, particularly with charcoal. It helps to infuse the food with that outdoor BBQ scent, plus I can make just about anything I would cook in my kitchen, only outside. That way, I can actually be with friends and family during the long grilling season.

So, I encourage you to keep an open mind here, and don't be afraid to try something new. When you're thinking, "Why on earth would I do a cheesecake in a Big Green Egg?" I'll tell you why—it's because you haven't tried cheesecake until you've tried my smoky Grilled Ricotta and Honey Cheesecake (page 232), cooked over charcoal on the aforementioned Big Green Egg.

This isn't just any average grill book. It's a mind-bending, eye-opening, ultimate bible that instructs you on how to do just about everything imaginable on the grill, from bubbling baked Brie (page 30) and Gochujang Honey Lime Wings (page 34) to Birria Tacos (page 170) and Grilled Strawberry Upside-Down Cake (page 217).

Now go stock up on your cast iron and get cooking.

THE BIG THREE

HOW TO IGNITE, MAINTAIN, AND USE YOUR GRILL, NO MATTER THE TYPE

WE'RE GOING TO MAKE SOME ASSUMPTIONS IN THIS BOOK. The first big one is that you know how to turn on your own grill. To that end, most recipes will simply start out by instructing to you to do so and preheat it, either for direct or indirect cooking, or in many cases, both. If by chance you're starting out with a new toy—say, shifting from gas to a Big Green Egg (our favorite for all things grilling), purchasing a smoker, or just looking for a more in-depth guide to using your grill—we have step-by-step instructions for you in this chapter. Once you master the basics here, you should be able to breeze through the recipes in this book without getting stuck on step one.

Though I have a yard full of every type of outdoor grilling vessel imaginable—including a caja china (essentially a big metal roaster box in which to build a firepit) and a cauldron—most people have one or some combination of the following three. If you can both perfect every which way of getting your grill hot and learn how to hold a specific temperature, you'll quickly master the art of grilling.

GAS VS. CHARCOAL

The biggest grillers' debate, of course, is whether to use a gas or charcoal grill. Purists will tell you that you can't beat the flavor of charcoal, but grill enthusiasts would say gas is much faster to set up and easier to use—simply turning a few knobs. They are both right.

Really, it comes down to personal preference. Most don't have space for both—and I always recommend buying as big of a grill as you can fit in your space—so pick your poison and run with it. The recipes in this book will work equally well on both.

GAS GRILL

Working with a gas grill is much like warming up your stovetop. Ignite the gas, adjust the temps, and get cooking. Typically, ten minutes or so of preheating are all you need to get your grill up to temperature. Before you start cooking, make sure you've cleaned off the grates with a grill brush to get rid of any residue, which will help prevent your food from sticking.

Since there are no coals to rake, you can adjust where you get heat based on how many burners you turn on. Rely on the attached thermometer or your own grill thermometer to keep an accurate reading, and use the knobs on the grill to control the temperature and maintain heat.

If you have a grill with three to six burners, think about how much surface area you actually need. Ignited burners will produce good direct heat, so if you're just cooking a couple pieces of chicken, light one or two burners and save the gas. If you're setting up for direct and indirect cooking, you'll want half turned on pretty high, and the other half left off. That leaves you with ambient heat on the indirect side, and a good searing surface on the direct side.

CHARCOAL GRILL

Before you start, always make sure your grill has been cleaned of ashes or old charcoal. Fill a chimney with your choice of charcoal or mesquite. The temperature you are trying to achieve will determine how much charcoal to light—the more charcoal, the higher the temp. The chimney will help the charcoal light faster by allowing air to move through the charcoal as well as feed the fire below it.

Place a fire starter or wadded-up newspaper underneath the chimney and ignite. Once the fire has started the charcoal, the bottom will begin to burn and rise up. When the fire reaches the top and the edges of the charcoal have begun to turn gray/white, it is time to dump the charcoal out.

Direct vs. Indirect

Indirect grilling is a smart and safe way to grill larger cuts or dishes, creating a hot side and a cold side of the grill so you're working with ambient heat as opposed to direct fire. You can either start or finish on the hot side, which will add hard high heat to your product, creating grill marks, more color, and more of a sear. The cold side will have radiant heat from the hot side and will allow your food to bake and reach that internal temperature you are looking for.

If cooking over indirect heat, you will need to dump or move the lit charcoal all onto one side of the grill,

creating a hot side, leaving the other side empty to create a cooler side.

If cooking over direct heat, spread into an even layer on the bottom of the grill for a more consistent single temperature.

Maintaining the Temperature in a Charcoal Grill

If grilling for a while, you will need to maintain the temperature of your grill. You can do this by adding more lumps of charcoal to the already hot coals.

Most grills have a temperature gauge installed on the lid of the grill. If using a grill that has a nonhinged lid, like a Weber kettle grill, make sure the thermometer on the lid is not sitting over the hot side of the grill if using the direct (hot side)/indirect (cool side) method. I like to use Bluetooth thermometers that can be placed inside the grill and will wirelessly let you know the exact temperature, notifying you when it increases or decreases.

If your heat is too great and you want to decrease the temperature, slightly close the bottom air vent. If your temperature is too low, open all the air vents completely, or add more fuel to the coals.

If you are looking to trap heat and slow down the increase of the temperature, slightly close the top air vent.

SMOKER

Before you get started, make sure the smoker is cleaned out and any of the grill racks you will be cooking on are clean.

As far as wood goes for the smoker, we like to use chunks versus chips. The chunks of wood will last longer and smolder whereas we found that the chips tend to burn up quicker. You can use oak, apple, cherry, or whatever you feel like pairing with your food. Wood chips are absolutely fine to use as well and are easier to find in a grocery store or supermarket. We recommend not soaking them in water, as the water will create steam before it creates any smoke. We also recommend using about 2 ounces (55 g) of smoking wood per 8 to 10 pounds (3.5 to 4.5 kg) of meat.

For a charcoal smoker, fill a chimney with your choice of charcoal or mesquite. Depending on the temperature you are trying to achieve, that will determine how much charcoal to light—the more charcoal, the higher the temp. The chimney will help the charcoal light faster by allowing air to move through the charcoal and air to feed the fire below it as well.

Place a fire starter or wadded-up newspaper underneath the chimney and ignite. Once the fire has started the charcoal, the bottom will begin to burn and rise up. Once you see the fire reach the top and the edges of the charcoal have begun to turn gray/white, it is time to dump the charcoal out. You do not want to ignite all the charcoal, especially if you are doing a long smoke. Ignite about one-quarter of the charcoal with the unlit charcoal bordering it. The heat will spread over time and ignite the other charcoal. Nestle the wood chunks into the lit and unlit charcoal.

If using a kettle-style grill to smoke on, dump the charcoal out into a pile on one side of the grill. Place a piece of foil folded like an upside-down T next to the pile to create a heat barrier. It will also help to place a small foil pan on the opposite side of the coals, to help catch any fat or drippings coming off the food you are smoking and prevent any grease from catching fire near the coals.

If using a ceramic grill to smoke on, fill the bottom with large lump charcoal or mesquite, and place

some of the chunks of smoking wood into it. Ignite the center of the charcoal and place a heat deflector (which will often come with your ceramic grill or can be purchased as an accessory) over the top. We recommend placing foil or some sort of drip tray on top of the heat deflector and then the grill grates over that.

If you are using an offset smoker, dump the charcoal into the charcoal box or area for the charcoal in the smoker.

At this point you want to close the lid to the smoker and watch what temperature you get to. You want it to be in the 225° to 250°F (107° to 121°C) range. Different smokers can be easier or harder to maintain the heat inside. Using a pellet or electric smoker means you won't have to babysit quite so much.

Once the desired heat has been achieved, sprinkle a few ounces or handfuls of the wood chips or chunks over the coals and close the door or lid. Too much wood can start a fire and add a bitter and astringent tinge to the flavor of the smoke. If you want to just slightly smoke something, use a small amount of wood.

Most smokers are all indirect heat, meaning the food you are smoking will never be sitting right next to or above the heat source. If you are using a kettle-style grill to smoke on, make sure to place the food you want to smoke away from the coals, on the "cold side" of the grill.

You're smoking! Now comes the hard part of maintaining the smoke and heat.

Maintaining the Temperature in a Smoker
As stated previously, most grills have a temperature gauge installed on the lid of the grill. I like to use Bluetooth thermometers that can be placed inside the grill and will wirelessly let you know the exact temperature, notifying you when it increases or decreases.

Once the heat you want is achieved, open the top air vent completely and close down the bottom air vent to about ⅛ inch (3 mm), if not less. This will control how much air is feeding the coals. Too much air will bring the heat up. Too little air will bring it down. The top air flow isn't allowing any air in, so that can remain open unless you are trying to cool the grill down or turn it off.

If your heat is too great and you want to decrease the temperature, close the bottom air vent completely or remove some of the coals. If your temperature is too low, open all the air vents a little, or add more charcoal to the coals. If you are looking to trap heat and slow down the increase of the temperature, slightly close the top air vent, but not completely.

In addition to adjusting the vents, adding more wood chips throughout cooking will keep the fire going, so be sure to have extra wood at the ready.

THE GRILLER'S ARSENAL

ACCESSORIES AND INGREDIENTS

ACCESSORIES

The first things you need to be successful as you work your way through grilling these recipes are a few good cast-iron pieces. But beyond that, it's important to have a handful of basic tools that you'll turn to time and again for outdoor grilling. In addition to the no-brainers—sheet pans for transporting food, grill brushes for dabbing on sauce or oil, spatulas and tongs with long handles—I've listed here a few of my favorite things to have at the ready when it's time to hit the grill.

Chimney Starter

If you're cooking with charcoal, a chimney starter—though not an absolute necessity—makes firing up the grill a million times easier. The cylindrical shape allows you to start your charcoal quickly and evenly without having to use lighter fluid, so you don't get any of that chemical burn-off.

SearPro Charcoal Torch Lighter

When you're lighting the grill, this is a game changer. The faster you can get the coals hot, the faster you can grill, and the strength of this flame will do the trick. Like the name suggests, this can also be used for searing meat and other ingredients right on the spot.

Grill Baskets

These are essential for fish and vegetables. When you're trying to get an entire meal done on the grill, a basket is great to have in your accessory collection. Some are open, like perforated bowls or woks that sit on the grill; some clamp together, keeping the ingredients inside. Either way, they keep smaller cuts of vegetables from falling through the grates and keep larger ingredients from sticking, while still getting the benefit of direct heat.

Skewers

You'll find a lot of recipes in the Apps and Grabs chapter (page 24) for skewers and kebabs, and it's great to have a couple of varieties of "sticks" in the house. I like having both a bag of wooden skewers that are disposable (but need a soak before going on the grill) and reusable metal ones, which are usually heftier, to hold bigger ingredients in a more stable way.

Spice Grinder

You can make any of the spice rubs in the Rubs chapter (page 236) using preground spices, but in my opinion, you'll get a completely different result if you start with whole spices—fennel seed, coriander seed, whole peppercorns. In their original form, they will release a fresh aroma and kicked-up flavor that sometimes gets dulled in a preground spice. Of course, for this you'll need either a really good mortar and pestle and some elbow grease, or a spice grinder. You can find a grinder for as little as $20 and you'll find yourself turning to it again and again.

Cast-Iron Flattop Griddle

A flattop griddle is worth having just for the Smash Burgers alone (page 100). As much as we love grill marks, sometimes you just need a good, even heat source that will offer solid support underneath your food. Beyond the burgers, use the flattop for fish, chicken, steak, or even pancakes.

Insulated Oven/BBQ Mitts

Especially if you are using cast iron on the grill, these are a must-own. Things get HOT when you're cooking over live fire, and sometimes a dish towel won't do the trick. Be sure you find something insulated, which will give you an added layer of protection.

Instant-Read Thermometer

By the time you become an experienced griller, you might be able to figure out the doneness of meat or fish by a touch test. For everyone else (and even for experienced chefs like me), it's imperative that you own a good digital thermometer. These will allow you to get a quick, accurate reading without having to cut into your food. Truly, if you own only one thing from this chapter, this should be it.

10- and/or 12-inch Cast-Iron Skillets

Anytime you're using your grill as an oven, these are necessary tools. A cast-iron skillet is as grill-safe as it gets, hold heats perfectly and evenly, and ensures a great crust or char on whatever you're cooking. Owning a couple of these skillets opens up your world significantly in terms of what you can actually cook on the grill. Best to get a 10-inch (25 cm) and/or a 12-inch (30 cm) skillet.

Cooler

Any smoking afficionado knows that the last key step to getting perfect texture on your barbecue is the final rest. Unlike letting a filet of beef or piece of chicken sit for 5 to 10 minutes, smoked meats typically need at least an hour of rest time. Sealing it in a cooler is the best way to do this, so it slows down the cooling time. Be sure you have a big-enough cooler to hold the meat without crowding.

Spray Bottle

This is for the smoking enthusiasts. If you have a smoker at home and love good low-and-slow-cooked food, you'll want to have a spray bottle on hand to hold

Smoker Spritz (page 239). The water and acid combo prevents your food from drying out as it cooks.

Butcher Paper

You shouldn't have a smoker without having some good butcher paper lying around. Most low-and-slow dishes like ribs, pork shoulder, and brisket benefit from being wrapped in the paper partway through cooking and put back in the smoker, which helps hold in fat and juices and speeds up cooking time. You can use aluminum foil in a pinch, but butcher paper allows more of the smoke to get through.

Cooling Rack/Perforated Grill Pan

Sometimes you just need one extra layer between your grates and your food to prevent sticking, and the cooling rack or perforated grill pan is the best accessory. I love cooking trout (see Grilled Whole Trout, page 113) on a wire cooling rack—make sure it's grill-safe; some are coated in plastic or rubber—and it makes for a fun presentation and quick, easy cooking. These types of perforated pans or crosshatched racks hold the food in a single layer and allow the heat from the grill to reach the food easily. It's also a great way to transport food—I use one almost as a grill-safe plate

that I can carry to the grill and then set it right on top.

Pizza Stone

Your grill can often be the best type of heat source for baking bread or making pizza, but you need a smooth, flat surface to get a sturdy bottom crust. That's where a good pizza stone comes in. By cooking bread products on the grill, you get a bit of smoky char that you wouldn't get otherwise, and the stone absorbs moisture as it cooks to create a crisp surface.

INGREDIENTS AND TIPS

There are some key ingredients and tips of the trade that are important to have and know about before you embark on this journey, like how to make grilled citrus (see below) for a garnish, the difference between steak finished with regular kosher salt and flaky Maldon sea salt (spoiler alert, the latter is better), and what I keep in my fridge to feel like I'm in a restaurant kitchen. Here are a few of my favorites.

Grilled Citrus Garnish

Not only does grilling your citrus make it that much juicier, but it's also a beautiful garnish that lets your guests know they're getting something delicious straight off the grill. To make it, rub a portion of the grill grates located over the hot side of the grill with oil. Place halved citrus—lemons, limes, oranges—cut-side down on the grill grates. Let cook until charred and caramelized, 2 to 5 minutes.

Maldon Flaky Sea Salt

What I like to think of as the finisher, this salt is a favorite for its coarse, flaky texture. It's both a flavor *and* a garnish. I love salt you can actually see, and feel between your teeth, and this one is a go-to. I use it on top of nearly every steak at Miller & Lux—a sprinkle of Maldon and a little oil are pretty much all you need to elevate a simple steak.

Charred Green Onions

Green onions are one of the easiest garnishes you can make and eat, and I like to throw a bunch on the grill when I'm making other food. The charred onions are the perfect accompaniment to meat, vegetables, fish, or any kind of Mediterranean or Asian dish.

Rosemary/Thyme Brush

When I'm brushing oil onto food or the grill grates, I love to gather a bunch of sturdy herbs like rosemary or thyme, tie them up with some kitchen twine (or another herb branch), and use that instead of a wad of paper towels or a regular grill basting brush. It will infuse a slight flavor into the oil and just looks nicer. It's the perfect way to use up extra herbs that you might not get to before they go bad in the fridge, and you can pop it on the platter as a rustic garnish after the food is done cooking.

Dijon Mustard

When you have nothing else but salt, pepper, oil, and acid (lemon juice, vinegar, etc.), Dijon mustard is the next ingredient that will take literally anything to a heightened level. I'll brush it on a whole tenderloin of beef, smear it on pork chops, spread it on salmon, or coat it on chicken. It's the definition of a pantry staple.

Peeled Garlic

We cook so often in my house that I always have a bag of already peeled garlic in the fridge. It's a restaurant kitchen trick that makes prep a million times easier, especially if you need multiple cloves in one meal. While I don't recommend buying the prechopped garlic in the jar, the peeled version totally passes the flavor test. Typically, when adding garlic to sauces or dressings, I'll blanch it for a few minutes in boiling water to eliminate some of the bite.

APPS AND GRABS

I SAY IT ALL THE TIME, AND I KNOW MOST PEOPLE AGREE—THE BEST PART OF ANY PARTY IS THE APPETIZERS. It's often where cooks get to flex their creativity and have a little fun experimenting with ingredient combos. In our Bay Area backyard, most of our gatherings start out with cocktails and hors d'oeuvres in a courtyard right below our vegetable garden. It's a really beautiful setting, and because I don't want to hide out in the kitchen and miss the party, I'll roll a grill over to the same area and set myself up so I can cook and visit with friends or family at the same time. That means apps (and all the things you can grab easily—think drumstick "lollipops," assorted skewers, and even grilled Brie with peaches and bread) come off the grill hot and ready to eat, and everyone can be a part of the action.

BARBECUE CHICKEN LOLLIPOPS

SERVES 5 OR 6

During one of our brainstorming sessions for the book, we were trying to figure out how to do "food on sticks" in some inventive ways. We decided a chicken bone totally counts as a stick, and these were born. The best part of this recipe is actually the Avocado BBQ Sauce (page 243), which I think of as Alabama white sauce meets California hippie. We haven't seen it anywhere else, and aside from ours being obviously green, it's creamy and earthy, perfect for serving with this hearty finger food. Great for everything from kid food to cocktail parties, this version of chicken on sticks might be our favorite preparation yet.

10 chicken drumsticks (about 2 pounds/
    910 g total)
3 tablespoons extra-virgin olive oil, plus more
    for the skillet
½ bunch thyme, leaves picked
Juice of 1 lemon
Kosher salt and freshly ground black pepper
1 cup (240 ml) chicken stock
1 cup (240 ml) Avocado BBQ Sauce
    (page 243)

To turn the chicken drumstick into "lollipops," start by frenching them. To do this, use a small knife to remove the tendon near the bottom (skinny part) of the drumstick. This should free the rest of the meat on the bone, and you can push all the meat to the top of the bone, making it look like a giant lollipop. Flip it and it should stand on its own. Repeat this step for all the drumsticks. Place all the cleaned and prepared chicken lollipops into a bowl and add the olive oil, thyme leaves, lemon juice, and salt and pepper to taste. Toss together until everything is evenly coated.

SET UP THE GRILL
Preheat a charcoal or gas grill to medium-high heat with a target temperature of 400°F (205°C). Place a large cast-iron skillet with a couple tablespoons of olive oil onto the hot grill to heat up.

Once hot, arrange the chicken in the pan around the outside with the bones sticking up. Cover the lid of the grill and cook for about 5 minutes.

Carefully add the chicken stock to the pan, close the lid of the grill again, and cook for 20 minutes more. The sauce on the bottom of the pan should be thick like gravy.

Serve the drumsticks with the avocado BBQ sauce for dipping.

GRILLED SHRIMP COCKTAIL

SERVES 4 TO 6

At my San Francisco steakhouse, Miller & Lux, we go big on seafood apps, since most people will opt for a meat-heavy main. The menu lists caviar donuts, kampachi tartare, an impressive three-tiered shellfish platter, and chilled Maine lobster with a creamy béarnaise sauce. And yet, what does nearly every table choose as part of their menu? You guessed it—the shrimp cocktail. It's hard to argue with something so simple and perfect. Here, I do quick charred shellfish straight off the grill. It's a quick and crowd-pleasing app, and one that even makes sense as a lighter main course.

For the cocktail sauce

½ cup (120 ml) ketchup

5 tablespoons prepared horseradish

2 tablespoons fresh lemon juice

2 tablespoons Worcestershire sauce

1 teaspoon hot sauce, such as Tabasco

¼ teaspoon kosher salt

⅛ teaspoon freshly ground black pepper

For the shrimp

1 pound (455 g) extra-jumbo shrimp (16/20), peeled and deveined

1 teaspoon kosher salt

1½ tablespoons extra-virgin olive oil

1 lemon, halved

1 tablespoon minced fresh parsley

1 tablespoon minced fresh chives

MAKE THE COCKTAIL SAUCE

In a bowl, add all the ingredients and whisk well to combine. Transfer to a small serving bowl and set aside until ready to use.

SET UP THE GRILL

Preheat a charcoal or gas grill to high heat with a target temperature of 500°F (260°C).

GRILL THE SHRIMP

Pat the shrimp dry on paper towels. If using frozen shrimp, make sure they are completely thawed and then pat dry. Season with the salt.

Pour the olive oil into a cast-iron skillet (see Note) and place the skillet on the grill. Once the pan is hot and the oil begins to shimmer and smoke, add the shrimp to the pan. Grill the shrimp for 2 minutes on one side. Flip the shrimp over and cook for another 2 minutes. While the shrimp is grilling, grease the grates, set the lemon cut-side down and grill until charred and caramelized, 2 to 5 minutes.

Remove the pan from the grill and sprinkle the parsley and chives into the pan. Serve the shrimp with the cocktail sauce and grilled lemon halves for squeezing.

Note: You could also cook the shrimp on skewers (soaked for at least 20 minutes, if wooden). Thread them on the skewers (two skewers for each row will allow you to easily flip the shrimp), brush with the olive oil, and grill straight on the grates for 2 minutes per side.

GRILLED BRIE WITH PEACHES AND HOT HONEY

SERVES 4

Baked Brie is one of those appetizers that feels fancy without having to put in a ton of effort. That's especially true when you throw it in a skillet on the grill, allowing the ambient heat to slowly cook the cheese. Top it however you like—here, I've paired it with semi-firm peaches that go right on the grates next to the skillet to get good grill marks, and are put in with the cheese at the end to finish cooking. Hot honey ups the ante in the best way.

For the hot honey

⅔ cup (165 ml) honey

1 small Fresno chile, finely minced

1 teaspoon minced fresh thyme, plus more for garnish

1 tablespoon fresh lemon juice

For the Brie and peaches

2 to 3 semi-ripe peaches, still somewhat firm, halved and pitted

6 tablespoons (90 ml) extra-virgin olive oil, divided, plus more for drizzling

1 6 to 8-ounce (170 to 225 g) wheel Brie or soft triple-cream cheese

For serving

½ pound (225 g) baguette, halved lengthwise and then cut into 2-inch pieces

Kosher salt

Thyme leaves, for garnish

MAKE THE HOT HONEY

In a small saucepan set over medium heat (either on a grill or stovetop), heat the honey until loosened and warm. Stir in the chile, thyme, and lemon juice until well combined. Set aside to let the flavors come together.

COOK THE PEACHES AND BRIE

Preheat a gas or charcoal grill to medium-high heat with a target temperature of 400°F (205°C).

While the grill is warming up, place a 10- to 12-inch (25 to 30 cm) cast-iron or grill-safe skillet on the grill to start heating. Once the skillet is hot, brush the halved peaches with 2 tablespoons olive oil and place cut side down on the skillet. Cook until the peaches are caramelized and slightly softened, 8 to 10 minutes. Flip the peaches over and cook another 5 to 6 minutes. Gently nudge the caramelized peaches to one side of the skillet, brush the Brie with 1 tablespoon of the oil, and add it to the skillet. Close the grill lid and cook for 5 minutes.

Meanwhile, brush the baguette slices with the remaining oil and sprinkle with salt. Place on the grill until toasted to your liking, taking care not to burn the bread.

Drizzle the cheese and peaches with half of the honey and some olive oil and cook until the cheese is gooey and warmed through and the peaches are quite softened and jammy, 8 to 10 more minutes.

ASSEMBLE THE DISH

Garnish with more hot honey, fresh thyme, and a sprinkle of salt and serve immediately with the crusty bread.

MEDITERRANEAN CAST-IRON CALAMARI

SERVES 4

Calamari is one of those ingredients that most prefer fried, but when it's
cooked properly without a crispy exterior, the finished product is much more
tender and elevated than you'd expect. That's what happens in this dish:
The calamari cooks in a cast-iron skillet in its own natural juices, bathed
in a garlicky, briny white wine sauce. Serve with crusty bread to soak up
the insanely good juices and you have a dish that works for anything from
app to main course.

2 pounds (910 g) calamari, tubes and
    tentacles

Kosher salt and freshly ground black pepper

3 tablespoons extra-virgin olive oil

4 cloves garlic, sliced

½ cup (75 g) salt-cured black olives

½ cup (120 ml) white wine

Pinch of chile flakes

1 tablespoon fresh marjoram leaves

1 small Fresno chile, thinly sliced

6 ounces (170 g) large cherry tomatoes on
    the vine (do not take them off the vine)

1 lemon, halved

Chopped fresh parsley, for garnish

Orange Chile Oil (page 240), for drizzling

Grilled bread, for serving

SET UP THE GRILL

Preheat a charcoal or gas grill to medium heat with a target
temperature of 350°F (175°C). As the grill is warming, place
a 10-inch (25 cm) cast-iron or grill-safe pan on the grates to
preheat.

Meanwhile, clean and dry the calamari well and season lightly
with salt and pepper.

Add the olive oil to the hot pan on the grill. When shimmering,
add the calamari and sauté until it begins to turn opaque, 3 to
4 minutes. Add the garlic and olives and stir to combine. Cook for
another 1 to 2 minutes to incorporate the flavors. Add the wine,
chile flakes, and marjoram leaves and cook down until the sauce
has thickened and the calamari is tender, 10 to 15 minutes. The
squid will also release some liquid as it is cooking down.

Season to taste with salt and black pepper, stir in the Fresno chiles,
and cook 1 to 2 minutes more.

While the calamari is cooking, place the cherry tomatoes right
on the grates and cook until slightly softened and charred, 4 to
5 minutes. Add the lemon halves to the grates and grill until nicely
charred and caramelized, 2 to 5 minutes.

When the calamari is ready, scatter the grilled tomatoes over
the top. Finish with some fresh parsley, a squeeze of fresh lemon
juice, and a drizzle of orange chile oil. Serve immediately with
grilled bread.

GOCHUJANG HONEY LIME WINGS WITH KIMCHI RANCH

SERVES 4

On game days and for big events, I'm always down for saucy Buffalo party wings, but when whole wings are going on the grill, I love the opportunity to have a little fun with flavors. This recipe is a nod to the Korean influences in the Bay Area and beyond. The hot sauce uses gochujang, which is Korean chile paste, along with honey and lime to coat the wings, and tangy kimchi ranch for dipping. Most grocery stores sell party wings already cut into drumettes and flats, so to get whole wings it's a good idea to call the butcher ahead of time and ask them to save some for you.

2½ pounds (1.2 kg) whole wings

3 cloves garlic, grated

4 teaspoons kosher salt

1 teaspoon sugar

¾ teaspoon freshly ground black pepper

¼ cup (60 ml) extra-virgin olive oil

Gochujang Honey Lime Sauce (page 239)

Kimchi Ranch (page 239)

Black sesame seeds, for garnish

Shiso leaves, for garnish

Chopped green onions, for garnish

Preheat the oven to 225°F (110°C); be sure not to have it on the convection setting. Line a sheet pan with parchment paper.

Place the chicken in a large bowl and add the garlic, salt, sugar, pepper, and olive oil. Mix well until everything is coated. Remove all the chicken from the bowl and place on the lined sheet pan.

Place the pan into the oven and bake until an instant-read thermometer reads 130°F (54°C), about 40 minutes. Remove from the oven to rest. At this point the chicken is partially cooked. You can place it in a zip-seal storage bag and store it for later use or freeze until needed.

When ready to serve, make the honey lime sauce and kimchi ranch as directed.

SET UP THE GRILL

Preheat a charcoal or gas grill to medium-high heat with a target temperature of 400°F (205°C).

While the grill is heating, toss the wings into the honey lime sauce until well coated.

Place the wings on the grill and cook, turning occasionally, until slightly charred and cooked through, about 12 minutes.

Garnish with sesame seeds, shiso leaves, and chopped green onions. Serve with the kimchi ranch for dipping.

CALABRIAN CHILE BUFFALO SHRIMP SKEWERS

SERVES 4 TO 6

In my vegetable garden, chile peppers grow in every variety, and over the years I've perfected a homemade hot sauce that's fermented with other Italian flavors (I call it Sicilian Slap). It's why I'll reach for Calabrian chiles at the store when I'm not using my own; for me, they're the closest thing, and I just love the hot-fresh flavor (as opposed to the hot-sour flavor) they produce.

For the Buffalo sauce

1 cup (225 g) sliced Calabrian chiles

1 stick (4 ounces/115 g) butter, at room temperature

3 tablespoons distilled white vinegar

2 tablespoons sriracha

1 tablespoon Worcestershire sauce

1 teaspoon onion powder

1 teaspoon garlic powder

1 teaspoon smoked paprika

1 teaspoon kosher salt

For the shrimp

2 pounds (910 g) jumbo shrimp, peeled and deveined

Metal or wooden skewers (soaked in water for at least 20 minutes if wooden)

For the blue cheese sauce

1 teaspoon extra-virgin olive oil

½ red onion, diced

½ teaspoon kosher salt

1 teaspoon red wine vinegar

½ cup (120 ml) sour cream

½ cup (120 ml) mayonnaise

½ cup (115 g) crumbled blue cheese

Juice of 1 lemon

2 teaspoons red wine vinegar

½ teaspoon onion powder

½ teaspoon garlic powder

1 teaspoon kosher salt

1 tablespoon minced fresh chives

For serving

Thinly shaved celery or celery sticks with the leaves, for garnish

Thinly sliced radishes, for garnish

MAKE THE BUFFALO SAUCE

In a blender, combine all the ingredients and puree until smooth. Set aside.

SET UP THE GRILL

Preheat a charcoal or gas grill to medium-high heat with a target temperature of 400°F (205°C). Grease the grates to prevent sticking.

PREPARE THE SHRIMP

Toss the shrimp in a bowl with some of the Buffalo sauce to coat it evenly. Skewer the shrimp on wood or metal skewers, placing each of the shrimp curled around the next, about 4 per skewer. Set aside while the grill heats up.

MAKE THE BLUE CHEESE SAUCE

Heat a medium sauté pan over medium heat. Add the oil and onion to the hot pan and sauté until the onions turn translucent, about 2 minutes, being careful not to caramelize them. Season with the salt. Deglaze with the vinegar and cook for 1 more minute, until they turn magenta in color and all the liquid has cooked off.

Transfer the cooled onions to a bowl. Add the rest of the ingredients to the bowl with the cooked onions and fold together with a spoon or spatula until evenly mixed. Set aside.

Place the skewers of shrimp on the grill and cook until the shrimp firm up and the Buffalo sauce begins to char a bit, about 2 minutes per side.

TO SERVE

Place the shrimp on a platter and brush a little more of the Buffalo sauce over them. Serve with a small bowl of the blue cheese dipping sauce and a little pile of shaved celery or celery sticks with the leaves and radish slices.

VIETNAMESE-STYLE BEEF SKEWERS

SERVES 6 TO 8

This blend of ginger, lemongrass, sambal oelek (chile paste), and sugar is inspired by flavors you can taste in Vietnamese cooking. This marinade creates a sweet and herbal glaze that, when grilled, has a sticky, almost candy-like quality, especially when whatever it coats is thinly sliced. These skewers would be just as good—and lighter, for an appetizer—without the rice, so feel free to omit that step as you build your lettuce wraps.

For the marinade

3 cloves garlic, peeled

1 knob ginger, peeled and roughly chopped

½ stalk lemongrass, cleaned and roughly
   chopped

1 teaspoon cumin seeds

1 teaspoon coriander seeds

Grated zest of 1 lime

2 tablespoons fish sauce

1 tablespoon sambal oelek

1 tablespoon hoisin sauce

1 tablespoon light brown sugar

1 teaspoon kosher salt

1 teaspoon freshly ground black pepper

For the beef skewers

2 pounds (910 g) beef filet, thinly sliced

8 wooden skewers, soaked in water for
   at least 20 minutes

For the nuoc cham sauce

¼ cup (50 g) sugar

¼ cup (60 ml) fish sauce

1 clove garlic, grated

1 teaspoon sambal oelek

Juice of 2 limes

For the ginger rice

2 cups (360 g) basmati rice

1 tablespoon (15 g) unsalted butter

½ tablespoon kosher salt

1 knob ginger, peeled and halved

For serving

1 head butter lettuce, cleaned and
   separated into leaves

1 bunch fresh mint

1 bunch fresh cilantro

1 cucumber, cut into matchsticks

1 carrot, cut into matchsticks

MAKE THE MARINADE

In a blender or food processor, combine ¼ cup (60 ml) water plus all the ingredients for the marinade and blend for 30 to 45 seconds to break up all the garlic, ginger, lemongrass, and seeds.

MARINATE THE BEEF

Spread all the sliced beef into a pan and pour the marinade over the top of it. Let sit for a few hours in the refrigerator, or up to overnight.

MAKE THE NUOC CHAM SAUCE

In a small pot, combine ½ cup (120 ml) water and the sugar and stir over medium heat until the sugar dissolves. Add the rest of the ingredients, stir to combine, and taste for seasoning. Set aside in the refrigerator until ready to use.

MAKE THE GINGER RICE

In a small pot, combine the rice, 3 cups (720 ml) water, the butter, salt, and ginger. Bring to a boil over high heat. Once boiling, reduce the heat to low, cover, and cook for 15 minutes. Uncover and fluff the rice with a fork.

SET UP THE GRILL

Preheat a charcoal or gas grill to medium-high heat with a target temperature of 400°F (205°C).

GRILL THE BEEF SKEWERS

Thread the beef slices across the skewers in an accordion pattern. Place the skewers on the grill and cook, rotating every 1 to 2 minutes, until they get a nice char and are cooked to your desired doneness, 6 to 7 minutes.

TO SERVE

For each serving, spoon some rice into the bottom of a plate or bowl. Place the skewers onto the plate with a few leaves of the butter lettuce, mint, cilantro, cucumber, and carrots. Serve with some of the nuoc cham sauce in a small ramekin or container for dipping.

To eat, place some rice, beef, carrots, cucumber, mint, and cilantro into one of the leaves of lettuce and roll up. Dip into the nuoc cham sauce.

BACON-WRAPPED SCALLOPS WITH CALABRIAN CHILE AIOLI

SERVES 2 TO 4

Scallops can be polarizing, but they're one of my favorite things to make for appetizers because those who like them typically *love* them, especially when wrapped in bacon. These are ridiculously easy to make and are particularly delicious because of the sauce, a spicy aioli made with jarred Calabrian chiles. Make a big batch of it—not only is it the perfect topper for the scallops, but it pairs well with everything from the Chicken Spiedini (page 43) and Grilled Shrimp Cocktail (page 29) to almost anything in the Steaks and Chops chapter.

For the Calabrian chile aioli

1 egg yolk

1¼ teaspoons kosher salt

1 teaspoon Dijon mustard

1½ tablespoons fresh orange juice

1 tablespoon jarred Calabrian chiles

1½ cups (360 ml) neutral oil, such as vegetable or grapeseed

For the scallops

12 sea scallops

6 slices bacon, halved

Kosher salt and freshly ground black pepper

3 tablespoons extra-virgin olive oil

12 toothpicks

For serving

1 orange, halved and grilled (see Grilled Citrus Garnish, page 21)

MAKE THE CALABRIAN CHILE AIOLI

In a blender, combine the egg yolk, salt, mustard, orange juice, and Calabrian chiles and puree until smooth. With the machine running, pour in the oil in a slow, steady stream until the aioli emulsifies. Thin with a tablespoon of water and taste for seasoning. Set aside until ready to use.

SET UP THE GRILL

Preheat a charcoal or gas grill to medium heat with a target temperature of 350°F (175°C). As the grill is warming, place a 12-inch cast-iron or grill-safe pan or cast-iron flattop griddle on the grates to preheat.

ASSEMBLE AND GRILL THE SCALLOPS

Pat the scallops dry with a paper towel and remove any side muscles. Wrap each scallop with half a slice of bacon around the edge and secure with a toothpick. Season with salt and pepper and drizzle with the olive oil.

Place the scallops into the hot pan and close the grill. Cook until well seared and almost cooked through, 3 to 4 minutes per side. Using tongs, turn the scallops on their sides and move around until the scallops are cooked through and the bacon is beginning to crisp.

Serve immediately with the grilled orange and the chile aioli for dipping.

CHICKEN SPIEDINI

SERVES 4 TO 6

The first time I had spiedini was on a trip years ago with Food Network to Florence and through Tuscany. One afternoon, we were in Montalcino filming at a winery. We stopped at a restaurant for an afternoon snack and aperitivo, and out came these impressive threaded appetizers. The server slid them off the skewers onto the plate and into a puddle of olive oil right in front of us, and we all happily dove in. I love that with this combo, each ingredient seasons the others—the pork fat drips onto the bread, bay leaves scent the chicken, and lemon juice drips down the skewers as they cook.

8 ounces (225 g) baguette

Extra-virgin olive oil, for brushing and drizzling

4 large or 8 small (see Note) metal or wooden skewers (soaked in water for at least 20 minutes if wooden)

1 pound (455 g) boneless, skin-on chicken thighs, cut into 12 pieces (1 to 2 inches/2.5 to 5 cm)

1 pound (455 g) cooked Italian sausage, cut into 12 pieces

12 large slices lemon (from 2 to 3 large lemons)

12 fresh bay leaves

Kosher salt and freshly ground black pepper

Orange Chile Oil (page 240), for drizzling

Sliced Thai bird's eye chiles, for garnish

Fresh marjoram, for garnish

SET UP THE GRILL

Preheat a charcoal or gas grill to medium-high heat, and set it up with two zones: a hot side and cold (less hot) side, for direct and indirect cooking. (See method, page 15.) You want the temperature to hover around 400°F (205°C).

While the grill is heating, assemble the skewers. Cut the baguette into sixteen ¼-inch (6 mm) slices and brush with some oil. Thread a piece of oil-brushed baguette onto each skewer, followed by a piece of chicken, a piece of sausage, a lemon slice, and a fresh bay leaf. Repeat two more times and end with a baguette slice. Brush the assembled skewers on all sides with olive oil, then season with salt and pepper.

Place on the hot side of the grill over direct heat for 3 to 4 minutes, just to get some char on the ingredients, flipping once after each minute to get all sides touched by the grill. Move the skewers over to the cooler side of the grill and cook over indirect heat for 10 minutes. Flip the skewers and cook another 8 minutes, until the chicken and sausage are cooked through.

Remove the skewers from the grill and finish with plenty of orange chile oil. Serve immediately, either on skewers or by pulling off the skewers and serving all together, family-style. Garnish with sliced Thai chiles and fresh marjoram.

Note: For appetizer-size portions, thread fewer ingredients on 8 smaller skewers.

PROSCIUTTO-WRAPPED FIGS WITH BALSAMIC

SERVES 4 TO 6 AS AN APPETIZER

This is one of those super-simple recipes that almost doesn't need to be written down. And it is always a hit. The dish works only when figs are in season, from about the end of July through the middle to end of September. The idea here is to get the fig soft on the inside while crisping up the prosciutto, all of which can be done in a few minutes on the grill. Using a thick, aged balsamic vinegar is important for the finish—you can also use a balsamic glaze if you prefer.

12 fresh figs

12 slices prosciutto

Extra-virgin olive oil, for drizzling

Aged balsamic vinegar, for drizzling

SET UP THE GRILL

Preheat a charcoal or gas grill to medium heat with a target temperature of 350°F (175°C).

While the grill is warming up, wrap each fig gently in a slice of prosciutto.

Place the figs directly on the grill, or thread onto skewers if preferred. Cook, turning occasionally, until the prosciutto is starting to become crispy and the figs feel soft when squeezed, 5 to 6 minutes.

Place the figs on a platter and drizzle with olive oil and aged balsamic vinegar.

OYSTER ROAST

SERVES 3 OR 4

Nestle large oysters on the half shell into a tray full of coarse salt to put on the grill for this quick recipe. The salt not only keeps the oysters stable, but helps distribute the heat evenly as they cook. The oyster butter, a blend of garlic, lemon, and parsley, can be made well in advance and lends just enough flavor to the briny shellfish. You can ask your seafood monger to shuck the oysters if you don't want to do it at home, but be sure to use them right away if that's the case.

For the oyster butter

1 stick (4 ounces/115 g) unsalted butter, at room temperature

2 teaspoons minced garlic

2 tablespoons chopped fresh parsley

Grated zest of 1 lemon

¾ teaspoon salt

½ teaspoon freshly ground black pepper

For the oysters

Kosher salt, for tray

1 dozen large oysters, shucked, on the half shell

1 lemon, halved

Grilled or toasted bread, for serving

MAKE THE OYSTER BUTTER

In a small bowl, stir the softened butter, garlic, parsley, lemon zest, salt, and pepper together until well blended.

SET UP THE GRILL

Preheat a charcoal or gas grill to medium-high heat with a target temperature of 400°F (205°C).

PREPARE THE OYSTERS

Spread enough kosher salt to coat a grill-safe sheet pan or baking dish (about 1 inch/2.5 cm thick). Nestle the oysters into the salt. Divide the oyster butter among the oysters, placing dollops on top.

Place the sheet pan on the grill and cook until the butter has melted and begins to bubble and the oysters are cooked through, 4 to 6 minutes. While the oysters are cooking, grease the grill grates, set the lemon halves cut side down on the grill, and grill until nicely charred and caramelized, 2 to 5 minutes.

Serve the oysters with grilled lemon for squeezing and with grilled or toasted bread.

Note: To shuck oysters at home, fold a kitchen towel in half lengthwise. Place the oyster in the middle of the towel and fold it over the top of the oyster, leaving the back of the oyster facing you. Place one hand on top of the towel, firmly holding the oyster in place. Using an oyster knife or "shucker," wedge the knife in the hinge (soft part) of the oyster, wiggling it until it goes all the way in. Slide the knife up against the lid, all the way to the mouth or front of the oyster, until the lid pops cleanly off. Now use the knife to free the oyster from the bottom of the cup, taking care not to spill the liquid "liquor." Flip the oyster over to show the "pretty side" and make sure the oyster is free from any bits of shell that may have broken off.

KĀLUA PORK AND PINEAPPLE SKEWERS

SERVES 4 TO 6

This is the perfect family-friendly recipe. Kids love the sticky teriyaki sauce and sweet grilled pineapple, and the adults will like the kick from the jalapeños. As with all the skewer recipes in the book, feel free to use what you have on hand and make this your own. I have giant sword-like sticks that I love to use for presentation, but I've made the assumption here that most are threading ingredients onto skinny wooden or metal skewers.

8 long wooden or metal skewers (soaked for at least 20 minutes if wooden)

1 small red onion, cut into 1-inch (2.5 cm) pieces

1¼ pounds (570 g) pork loin, cut into 24 chunks (1 inch/2.5 cm)

1 pineapple, cut into 24 chunks (1 inch/2.5 cm)

3 to 4 large jalapeño peppers, cut into 16 pieces (1 inch/2.5 cm)

Extra-virgin olive oil, for brushing

Kosher salt and freshly ground black pepper

Teriyaki Sauce (page 241)

Fresh cilantro, for garnish

SET UP THE GRILL

Preheat a charcoal or gas grill to medium-high heat with a target temperature of 400°F (205°C).

On each skewer, thread 2 petals of red onion, followed by a piece of pork, then pineapple, then jalapeño. Repeat two more times, but don't put a jalapeño at the end—finish with a pineapple chunk. Brush the skewers with olive oil and season well with salt and pepper.

Grill the skewers directly on the grates, turning occasionally, until the pork is cooked through and the onions, pineapple, and jalapeños are slightly charred, 7 to 8 minutes total. Each time you turn the skewers, brush with some teriyaki sauce.

Serve hot with extra teriyaki sauce, for dipping. Garnish with cilantro.

CAST-IRON GRILLED TUNA TATAKI

MAKES 6 LETTUCE CUPS

We pulled out the cast-iron flat griddle pan for this fun starter, which just slightly chars raw tuna right on the surface. You can easily turn this into more of a main dish by serving the tuna over rice with the cucumber mixture, some diced avocado, vegetables of your choice, and the unagi sauce on top.

For the unagi sauce

¼ cup (55 g) sugar

¾ cup (180 ml) mirin

¼ cup (60 ml) sake

1 ounce (28 g) fresh ginger, grated

¾ cup (180 ml) reduced-sodium soy sauce or tamari

1 tablespoon plus 1 teaspoon cornstarch, mixed with 2 tablespoons plus 2 teaspoons water to make a slurry

Juice of ½ lemon

For the tuna lettuce cups

16 ounces (455 g) ahi tuna, center-cut loin

1 tablespoon extra-virgin olive oil

Kosher salt and freshly ground black pepper

1 small cucumber, sliced thin

2 green onions, light and dark green parts, thinly sliced

1 Fresno chile, cut into thin rings

2 tablespoons rice wine vinegar

1 tablespoon mirin

6 large shiso leaves

6 leaves butter lettuce

White and black sesame seeds, for garnish

MAKE THE UNAGI SAUCE

In a small pot, combine the sugar, mirin, sake, and ginger and bring to a boil over medium heat. Once boiling, add the soy sauce and simmer for 10 minutes. Add the cornstarch slurry and bring to a boil to thicken into a glaze. Season with lemon juice.

GRILL THE TUNA

Preheat a charcoal or gas grill to medium-high heat, with a target temperature of 400°F (205°C). While the grill is heating, place a cast-iron griddle on the grates. Rub the tuna with the oil and lightly season with salt and pepper. Sear the tuna slab for 30 to 45 seconds per side, or until golden brown. Sear all four sides evenly, leaving the center of the tuna raw. Let rest for 2 to 3 minutes before slicing. Slice the tuna against the grain, about the thickness of a pencil.

ASSEMBLE THE TUNA LETTUCE CUPS

Place the cucumber, green onions, fresno chile, rice wine vinegar, and mirin into a bowl with a pinch of salt and mix together. Set aside.

Place a large shiso leaf in each cup of lettuce, top with a slice of tuna, and add a bit of the cucumber mixture. Serve with the unagi sauce.

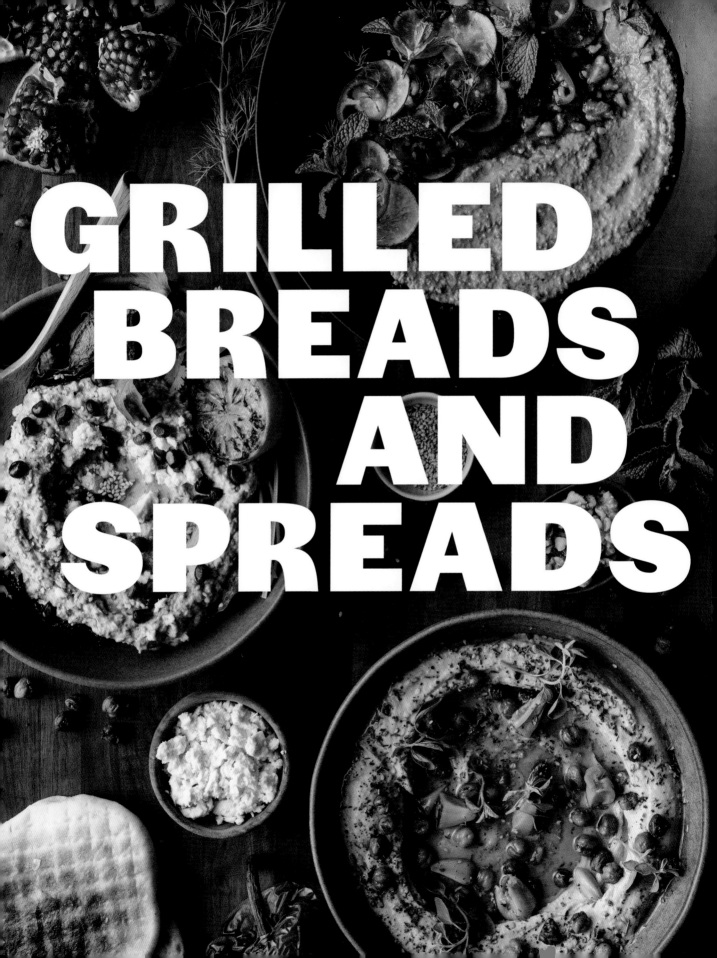

GRILLED BREADS AND SPREADS

IMAGINE SETTING UP A WHOLE MEDITERRANEAN SPREAD FOR DINNER, like the Beef Kofta with Grilled Eggplant (page 120), and instead of tucking it all into sad, flat pockets of store-bought pita, you produce your own homemade pita right on the grill at the same time. In an instant, you've upped the ante in a very simple but monumental way.

That's what this chapter is all about: not necessarily the full meals, but the fun grazing add-ons that go with them. I particularly love the updated version of an old-school cheese ball (this one made with grilled salmon, charred green onions, and everything bagel seasoning) and the hummus, baba ghanoush, and muhammara trio, all of which incorporate fun grilled elements and can be served with a variety of breads or dippers.

This isn't to say that you won't find dinner in this chapter. You can for sure put together a fun pizza night and let everyone get involved in the toppings, and the Grilled Pork Store Special (page 70) might just be one of my favorite recipes in the book. It was inspired by some late-night social media scrolling, and we made the open-faced grilled pork sandwich our own by adding a few fun touches. Ahead are the tried-and-true recipes that you'll tuck away to accompany other great dishes in the book for dinner party menus.

PIZZA DOUGH

MAKES ENOUGH FOR FOUR 12-INCH (30 CM) PIZZAS

It's essential to have a perfected pizza dough recipe in your repertoire, and it's much simpler than you might think. This one has an ethereal lightness to the dough itself that comes from tipo "00" flour and a high moisture content. The texture allows you to get those bubbles that burst and char on the grill as it cooks. You can buy tipo "00" flour in the baking aisle of most grocery stores, but all-purpose is a fine substitute if you can't find it—the dough just won't be quite as light.

10 ounces (280 g) all-purpose flour

10 ounces (280 g) tipo "00" flour

11 ounces water (310 g) at 100° to 105°F
    (38° to 40°C)

¼ teaspoon active dry yeast

2 tablespoons neutral oil

1 tablespoon honey

1 tablespoon kosher salt

Semolina flour, for dusting

In a stand mixer fitted with the dough hook, combine the all-purpose flour, "00" flour, water, yeast, oil, and honey and beat on the lowest speed for 2 minutes. Add the salt to the bowl and mix on speed 2 for 10 minutes.

Grease a large container with a lid or a bowl with cooking spray or olive oil. Place the dough ball into the container and spray the top of it with more oil. Place an airtight lid on the container (or if in a bowl, cover well with plastic wrap). Place the dough in a warm spot until doubled in size, about 1 hour.

Once doubled in size, remove the dough from the container and portion it into four 8-ounce (225 g) dough balls. Roll the dough balls in a circular motion until they are smooth all the way around and there are no creases.

Spray a sheet pan with cooking spray and dust it with semolina flour. Place the dough balls on the pan and spray the tops with cooking spray or oil. Gently drape plastic wrap over the top of the dough, edge to edge, so that it does not dry out or restrict the dough from rising.

At this point you can leave the dough out on the counter until doubled in size again. Or place it in the refrigerator up to overnight for use later or the next day.

GRILLED MARGHERITA PIZZA

MAKES ONE 12-INCH (30 CM) PIZZA

The biggest obstacle to pizza night is having everything out hot and ready at the same time. My solution is to blind bake (or grill) the crust—i.e., cook it partway—then have people top the precooked dough however they like. That way, they just need time for cheese to melt and toppings to heat up, and everything is good to go around the same time. I'll typically watch other people go overboard with toppings, but for me, it's margherita every time. The simple combo of sauce, mozzarella, and basil is the perfect trifecta—there's a reason it's the most famous trio.

Flour or cornmeal, for dusting

8 ounces (225 g) pizza dough, store-bought or homemade (page 54)

¾ cup (180 ml) Pizza Sauce (page 242)

4 ounces (115 g) fresh mozzarella cheese

Extra-virgin olive oil, for brushing and drizzling

Kosher salt

Fresh basil leaves

Freshly grated Parmigiano-Reggiano cheese, for garnish

SET UP THE GRILL

Preheat a charcoal or gas grill to very high heat with a target temperature of 650°F (340°C). While the grill is heating up, place a pizza stone on top of the grates to get it very hot.

GRILL THE PIZZA

Dust a pizza peel or the back of a baking sheet with flour or cornmeal to prevent sticking. Stretch and shape the dough into a flat round about 12 inches (30 cm) in diameter and place on top of the peel or pan. Spread the pizza sauce over the dough, leaving about 1 inch (2.5 cm) around the edges free of sauce for the crust. Tear or slice the mozzarella and scatter evenly over the sauce. Brush the edges with extra-virgin olive oil and drizzle a little bit over the top of the pizza. Sprinkle with salt.

Carefully slide the pizza onto the hot stone on top of the grill. Cover and cook until the crust is puffed and golden and the middle is cooked through, 3½ to 5 minutes. You can also check the dough by lifting the pizza up slightly with the peel and checking on the bottom of the crust. Once the bottom is a dark golden brown, it is ready.

Remove from the grill and immediately scatter fresh basil and some freshly grated Parmigiano-Reggiano over the top. Finish with more oil and salt, if desired.

MIXED WILD MUSHROOM, BRIE, AND SAGE PIZZA

MAKES ONE 12-INCH (30 CM) PIZZA

Use any variety of wild mushrooms you can find for this earthy, creamy pizza, which pairs a base of béchamel with Brie cheese and sage scents. I love maitakes for their wispy edges that crisp as they cook, but even regular cremini mushrooms would do the job here. This is a year-round pizza, though I particularly like it in the early fall, when the season is turning and I want something a little more substantial.

¼ pound (115 g) mixed wild mushrooms

1 tablespoon extra-virgin olive oil, plus more for drizzling

Kosher salt and freshly ground black pepper

1 teaspoon chopped fresh thyme, plus more for garnish

Flour or cornmeal, for dusting

8 ounces (225 g) pizza dough, store-bought or homemade (page 54)

¾ cup (180 ml) Béchamel (page 242)

3 ounces (85 g) Brie cheese, thinly sliced

A few fresh sage leaves

Parmigiano-Reggiano cheese, for grating

Grated lemon zest, for garnish

SAUTÉ THE MUSHROOMS

Clean the mushrooms of any dirt or debris. Heat a skillet over medium heat and add the oil. When shimmering, add the mushrooms. Sauté for 3 to 4 minutes until slightly softened, stirring occasionally. Season with salt and pepper and stir in the thyme. Set aside.

SET UP THE GRILL

Preheat a charcoal or gas grill to very high heat with a target temperature of 650°F (340°C). While the grill is heating up, place a pizza stone on top of the grates to get it very hot.

GRILL THE PIZZA

Dust a pizza peel or the back of a baking sheet with flour or cornmeal to prevent sticking. Stretch and shape the dough into a flat round about 12 inches (30 cm) in diameter and place on top of the peel or pan. Spread the béchamel over the dough, leaving about 1 inch (2.5 cm) around the edges free of sauce for the crust. Spread the mushrooms evenly over the sauce and scatter the Brie in and around the mushrooms.

Carefully slide the pizza onto the hot stone on top of the grill. Cover and cook until the crust is puffed and golden, the cheese is melted, and the middle is cooked through, about 5 minutes. In the last minute of cooking, scatter a few sage leaves over the top of the pizza.

Remove from the grill and immediately grate Parmigiano-Reggiano over the top, along with fresh lemon zest and a little more thyme. Finish with more oil and salt, if desired. Serve hot.

PINEAPPLE, HAM, AND JALAPEÑO PIZZA

MAKES ONE 12-INCH (30 CM) PIZZA

There are two kinds of people in this world—those who like pineapple on their pizza and those who are, well, boring. Just saying. For real, though, the whole pineapple/ham thing is just about balance: having sweet and salty elements that complement each other and make you want to go back in for another bite, especially with the added layer of spicy jalapeño.

Flour or cornmeal, for dusting

8 ounces (225 g) pizza dough, store-bought or homemade (page 54)

¾ cup (180 ml) Pizza Sauce (page 242)

⅔ cup (75 g) grated Monterey Jack cheese

¼ pineapple, cored and sliced into thin rings

2 slices cooked ham, torn into pieces

½ jalapeño pepper, cut into thin rings

Minced fresh parsley, for garnish

Arugula, for garnish

Parmigiano-Reggiano cheese, for grating

Extra-virgin olive oil, for drizzling

Kosher salt

SET UP THE GRILL

Preheat a charcoal or gas grill to very high heat with a target temperature of 650°F (340°C). While the grill is heating up, place a pizza stone on top of the grates to get it very hot.

GRILL THE PIZZA

Dust a pizza peel or the back of a baking sheet with flour or cornmeal to prevent sticking. Stretch and shape the dough into a flat round about 12 inches (30 cm) in diameter and place on top of the peel or pan. Spread the pizza sauce over the dough, leaving about 1 inch (2.5 cm) around the edges free of sauce for the crust. Scatter the cheese over the sauce evenly. Arrange the pineapple evenly over the cheese. Place pieces of ham in and around the pineapple. Top with jalapeño rings.

Carefully slide the pizza onto the hot stone on top of the grill. Cover and cook until the crust is puffed and golden, the cheese is melted, and the pineapple has softened slightly, about 5 minutes.

Remove from the grill and immediately garnish with fresh parsley and arugula leaves. Grate Parmigiano-Reggiano over the top. Add a drizzle of olive oil and a sprinkle of salt to taste. Serve hot.

SAUSAGE, BROCCOLI RABE, AND CALABRIAN CHILE PIZZA

MAKES ONE 12-INCH (30 CM) PIZZA

If I'm ordering two pizzas at a restaurant, I'll get one margherita, and then I'll get something like this, one of my all-time favorite combos. Sausage and broccoli rabe are the perfect pairing, as the bitter greens cut the fat of the sausage. It's a common Italian pasta sauce but is great as a pizza topper, too. Also on this one is a double-chile kick—the perfect zing from Calabrian chiles and homemade orange chile oil, both of which complement the rustic and super-savory flavor profile of this pie.

Kosher salt

½ bunch broccoli rabe

1 tablespoon extra-virgin olive oil

1 sweet Italian sausage, casing removed

Flour or cornmeal, for dusting

8 ounces (225 g) pizza dough, store-bought
　　or homemade (page 54)

¾ cup (180 ml) Béchamel (page 242)

2 tablespoons jarred Calabrian chiles,
　　or to taste

Parmigiano-Reggiano cheese, for grating

Orange Chile Oil (page 240), for drizzling

SET UP THE GRILL

Preheat a charcoal or gas grill to very high heat with a target temperature of 650°F (340°C). While the grill is heating up, place a pizza stone on top of the grates to get it very hot.

Meanwhile, bring a large pot of well-salted water to a boil. Add the broccoli rabe and cook until tender, 5 to 7 minutes. Drain and rinse under cold water, then squeeze out excess moisture. Set aside.

In a small skillet, warm the olive oil over medium heat until hot but not smoking. Add the sausage and sauté, breaking up with a wooden spoon, until cooked through, 6 to 8 minutes. Set aside.

GRILL THE PIZZA

Sprinkle a pizza peel or the back of a baking sheet with flour or cornmeal to prevent sticking. Stretch and shape the dough into a flat round about 12 inches (30 cm) in diameter and place on top of the peel or pan. Spread the béchamel over the dough, leaving about 1 inch (2.5 cm) around the edges free of sauce for the crust. Scatter the broccoli rabe and sausage evenly over the sauce.

Carefully slide the pizza onto the hot stone on top of the grill. Cover and cook until the crust is puffed and golden, the béchamel is bubbling, and the middle is cooked through, about 5 minutes. In the last minute of cooking, spoon the Calabrian chiles over the pizza, as desired.

Remove from the grill and immediately grate Parmigiano-Reggiano over the top. Finish with a drizzle of orange chile oil and salt to taste. Serve hot.

CHOPPED SALAD PIZZA

MAKES ONE 12-INCH (30 CM) PIZZA

This recipe was inspired by one my producer, Amanda Gold, grew up eating. She spent some of her high school years in Connecticut slinging pies (Mystic Pizza vibe and all) and swore that the house Italian iceberg salad made a better pizza topper than just about anything else. We developed a salad recipe that feels a little more in line with an Italian chopped salad of today, and we loved the outcome. If you're going through the effort to do all the slicing and dicing for the chopped salad, consider making multiple pizzas here.

3 cups Italian Chopped Salad (recipe follows)

Flour or cornmeal, for dusting

8 ounces (225 g) pizza dough, store-bought or homemade (page 54)

¾ cup (120 ml) Pizza Sauce (page 242)

Grated Parmigiano-Reggiano cheese, for serving

SET UP THE GRILL

Preheat a charcoal or gas grill to very high heat with a target temperature of 650°F (340°C). While the grill is heating up, place a pizza stone on top of the grates to get it very hot.

GRILL THE PIZZA

Dust a pizza peel or the back of a baking sheet with flour or cornmeal to prevent sticking. Stretch and shape the dough into a flat round about 12 inches (30 cm) in diameter and place on top of the peel or pan. Spread the pizza sauce over the dough, leaving about 1 inch (2.5 cm) around the edges free of sauce for the crust.

Carefully slide the pizza crust onto the hot stone on top of the grill. Cover and cook until the crust is puffed and golden and the sauce has a slightly cooked look, about 5 minutes.

Remove from the grill and pile the salad on top of the sauce. Garnish with Parmigiano-Reggiano cheese and serve immediately.

ITALIAN CHOPPED SALAD

SERVES 6

This salad holds up well in the fridge for at least 24 hours.

For the salad dressing

¼ cup (60 ml) red wine vinegar

1 tablespoon Dijon mustard

1 clove garlic, minced

½ cup (50 g) grated Parmigiano-Reggiano cheese

1½ teaspoons dried oregano

½ cup (120 ml) extra-virgin olive oil

Kosher salt and freshly ground black pepper

For the chopped salad

1 head romaine lettuce, thinly sliced

1 head radicchio, thinly sliced

6 ounces (170 g) provolone cheese, finely diced

3 ounces (85 g) salami, cut into matchsticks

1 small red onion, sliced thin

1 cup (155 g) pitted Castelvetrano olives, quartered

½ cup (60 g) sliced pepperoncini

MAKE THE DRESSING

In a screw-top jar, combine the vinegar, mustard, garlic, Parmigiano-Reggiano, oregano, and oil and shake vigorously until well combined. Season to taste with salt and pepper.

PREPARE THE SALAD

In a large bowl, toss the salad ingredients together. Add the desired amount of dressing to the salad and toss (you may not use all the dressing).

GRILLED PITA BREAD

MAKES 8 PITA ROUNDS

Few things are more depressing to me than the bagged flat pita rounds you find at the grocery store. And though it's not super difficult to find a restaurant or outlet making fluffier ones, I find that if you're planning to fire up the grill anyway, it's no big deal to make your own. This simple dough requires only one 90-minute rise—and they'll cook up in under 5 minutes on the grill. It's one of those things that will blow guests away with minimal effort on your part. Once you do it, you won't want to visit that section of the bread aisle again.

1 envelope (¼ ounce/7 g) active dry yeast

1 teaspoon sugar

1½ cups (360 ml) warm water

2 teaspoons kosher salt

3½ cups (472 g) bread flour, plus more for dusting

1 teaspoon extra-virgin olive oil, for the bowl

In the bowl of a stand mixer, stir together the yeast, sugar, and warm water to blend. Let the mixture stand until the yeast is foamy, 5 to 10 minutes.

Stir in the salt. Snap on the dough hook. Add the flour, a little at a time, mixing at the lowest speed until all the flour has been incorporated and the dough gathers into a ball; this should take about 4 minutes.

Place the dough on a lightly floured surface and knead until it's smooth and elastic. Transfer the dough to a lightly oiled bowl, turn it over to coat, and cover with plastic wrap. Allow to rise until doubled in size, about 1½ hours.

MEANWHILE, SET UP THE GRILL

Preheat a charcoal or gas grill to high heat with a target temperature of 500°F (260°C). While the grill is heating up, place a pizza stone on top of the grates to get it very hot.

Punch the dough down, divide it into 8 portions, and gather each piece into a ball. Keep all of them lightly floured and covered while you work. Allow the balls of dough to rest, covered, for 15 minutes so they will be easier to roll out.

Using a rolling pin, roll each dough ball into a round or oval that is about 8 inches (20 cm) in diameter or length and ¼ inch (6 mm) thick. Make sure the round is totally smooth, with no creases or seams in the dough, which can prevent the pitas from puffing up properly. Cover the disks as you roll them out, but do not stack them up.

Put 2 pitas at a time on the hot pizza stone and bake until the bread puffs up like a balloon and is pale golden, 3 to 4 minutes. Watch closely; they bake fast. Remove the bread from the grill and place on a rack to cool for 5 minutes. They will naturally deflate, leaving a pocket in the center. Wrap the pitas in a large kitchen towel to keep them soft.

GRILLED TOMATO, OLIVE, AND ROSEMARY FOCACCIA BREAD

SERVES 6 TO 8

If you're into fresh baked bread, there's nothing easier than focaccia. It's the jumping-off point for novice bread bakers, and I love the visual appeal of this one. Fat, juicy cherry tomatoes on the vine, which are tucked into the dimples of the focaccia dough, will slightly burst as the bread cooks on the grill. Cut this up and serve it alongside the Mediterranean Cast-Iron Calamari (page 33) or Grilled Clams Casino (page 110)—it's the perfect sponge to drag through each sauce.

2 teaspoons instant (rapid-rise) yeast

1 cup (240 ml) warm water (100° to 105°F/ 38° to 40°C)

2 tablespoons sugar

3½ to 4 cups (438 to 500 g) AP flour

1 tablespoon kosher salt

¼ cup (60 ml) extra-virgin olive oil, plus more for the bowl and pan

Cornmeal, for dusting

For the toppings

2 tablespoons extra-virgin olive oil

1 bunch cherry tomatoes on or off the vine (about 8 ounces/225 g)

10 Kalamata olives, pitted and quartered

2 tablespoons fresh rosemary

Maldon or other coarse sea salt

Freshly ground black pepper

In the bowl of a stand mixer, combine the yeast, warm water, and sugar and stir gently to dissolve. Let stand 3 to 5 minutes until foamy.

Snap on the dough hook, turn the mixer on low, and slowly add the flour to the bowl.

Dissolve the salt in 2 tablespoons water and add it to the dough. Pour in the olive oil. When the dough starts to come together, increase the speed to medium. Stop the machine periodically to scrape the dough off the hook. Mix until the dough is smooth and elastic, about 10 minutes, adding flour as necessary.

Turn the dough out onto a work surface and fold over itself a few times. Form the dough into a ball and place in an oiled bowl. Turn to coat the entire ball with oil so it doesn't form a skin. Cover with plastic wrap or a damp towel and let rise in warm place until doubled in size, 45 minutes to 1 hour.

Coat a grill-safe 9 by 13-inch (23 by 33 cm) quarter-sheet pan or similar size cast-iron pan with a little olive oil and dust with cornmeal. Once the dough is doubled and domed, turn it out onto the counter. Roll and stretch the dough out to the shape of the pan, about ½ inch (1.3 cm) thick. Lay the flattened dough on the pan and cover with plastic wrap. Let rest for 30 minutes until risen again.

MEANWHILE, SET UP THE GRILL

Preheat a charcoal or gas grill to medium-high heat, and set it up with two zones: a hot side and cold (less hot) side, for direct and indirect cooking. (See method, page 15.) You want the temperature to hover around 400°F (205°C).

Uncover the dough and press to dimple with your fingertips. Brush the surface with olive oil, place the tomatoes inside indents in the dough, scatter the olives and rosemary evenly, and sprinkle on salt and pepper to taste. Place on the cool side of the grill and cook, rotating the pan every 10 minutes, until golden and cooked through with an internal temperature of 210°F (100°C), about 30 minutes.

Let rest for at least 45 minutes before serving.

GRILLED PORK STORE SPECIAL

SERVES 4

This is my version of the pressed sausage loaf, several varieties of which I saw on one of my social media deep dives one night. Ours was given a fancy new name—who doesn't want to order something called Pork Store Special?—and gets a peppery bite from an arugula garnish and a hit of heat from homemade citrus chile oil, though any chile oil will be great.

6 ounces (170 g) provolone cheese, shredded

½ long (2 foot) Italian loaf, split

1¼ pounds (570 g) Italian sausage, casings removed

2 to 3 tablespoons extra-virgin olive oil

Orange Chile Oil (page 240), for drizzling

Baby arugula, for garnish

Pizza Sauce (page 242), for serving

SET UP THE GRILL

Preheat a charcoal or gas grill to medium-high heat with a target temperature of 400°F (205°C). While the grill is heating up, place a cast-iron flattop griddle on the grates to get it very hot.

Evenly spread the provolone out on the cut sides of the bread. Press the sausage meat on top of the cheese, pushing it down so it adheres to the bread in an even layer. Brush the top of the sausage with the olive oil.

Carefully place the sausage bread on the griddle, sausage side down. Cook until the sausage is browned, crisp, and cooked all the way through and the cheese is melted, 6 to 8 minutes. Flip the bread and toast on the other side, 3 to 4 minutes more.

Remove from the grill, drizzle with orange chile oil, and garnish with arugula. Cut into slices and serve hot, with pizza sauce on the side for dipping.

GRILLED EGGPLANT BABA GHANOUSH

MAKES 2 CUPS (480 ML)

Baba ghanoush is my favorite thing to make with eggplant in the summertime—and really, the only thing I want to make with eggplant in the summertime. There are only so many ways you can use the deep purple vegetable, and grilling slices often means it's leathery and brown by the time it comes off the grill. Leaving it whole on the grates produces a caramelized, meaty flesh that can be whipped into a light and creamy spread with the addition of just a few easy pantry staples.

2 large globe eggplants

⅓ cup (75 ml) tahini

1 clove garlic, grated

½ teaspoon ground cumin

Juice of 1 lemon, or to taste

Kosher salt and freshly ground black pepper

Optional garnishes: fresh mint, fresh cilantro, pomegranate seeds, pine nuts

SET UP THE GRILL

Preheat a charcoal or gas grill to medium-high heat with a target temperature of 400°F (205°C).

Using a fork or the tip of a knife, poke a few holes in the eggplant to release steam. Grill until softened and puckered, 25 to 30 minutes.

When the eggplants are cool enough to handle, spoon the flesh into a bowl, discarding excess liquid. Discard the skins. Add the tahini, garlic, cumin, and lemon juice. Whisk everything together until smooth. Season to taste with salt and pepper. Garnish as desired.

MUHAMMARA

MAKES 2 CUPS (480 ML)

I often think of muhammara as the forgotten stepchild of Mediterranean spreads—
not as popular or necessary as hummus or tzatziki, not as familiar as baba
ghanoush or garlicky toum. But it would be a shame to overlook this earthy,
jewel-toned blend, which gets sweetness from roasted peppers and pomegranate
molasses, richness from walnuts, and bright acidity from lemon juice.

4 red bell peppers

1 cup (100 g) walnuts

2 tablespoons pomegranate molasses

1 tablespoon fresh lemon juice, plus more
    to taste

1 tablespoon Aleppo pepper, plus more
    to taste

1 tablespoon paprika, plus more to taste

½ teaspoon ground cumin

1 teaspoon kosher salt, plus more to taste

3 tablespoons extra-virgin olive oil, plus
    more as needed

Optional garnishes: fresh mint, dill, shaved
    radishes, sliced Fresno chiles, ground
    walnuts

SET UP THE GRILL

Preheat a charcoal or gas grill to medium-high heat with a target
temperature of 400°F (205°C).

Place the red peppers directly on the grates. Use tongs to turn the
peppers every 2 to 3 minutes until they are completely blackened
and charred, 10 to 12 minutes total. Immediately place the
peppers in a heatproof bowl and cover them tightly with plastic
wrap. Set aside for 5 to 10 minutes to steam the peppers and
loosen the skin.

Once cooled down a bit, remove the skin with your fingers or paper
towels. Slice the peppers open and remove the stems, membrane,
and seeds. Roughly chop the peppers and set aside.

In a blender or food processor, combine the walnuts, pomegranate
molasses, lemon juice, Aleppo pepper, paprika, cumin, and
1 teaspoon kosher salt and process until smooth.

Add the chopped peppers and continue to process until smooth
and creamy. With the blender running, add the olive oil in a thin
stream. If too thick, thin the dip by adding a tablespoon of water at
a time until the desired consistency is reached. Season with salt to
taste. Add more lemon juice, Aleppo pepper, or paprika to taste.

Let the flavors develop for a few hours in the refrigerator and serve
with garnishes of your choice.

WHITE MISO HUMMUS WITH GRILLED LEMON AND GARLIC

MAKES 2 CUPS (480 ML)

This recipe came to be when we were exploring ways to add a unique flavor profile to a dish that's been done to death. Could we do a simple grill-roasted garlic hummus? Sure, but we thought it would be more fun to add an element of surprise with a spoon of white miso, which adds caramel umami tones and elevates the chickpea spread into something with depth and richness.

1 head garlic

¼ cup (60 ml) extra-virgin olive oil, plus more for drizzling

Kosher salt

1 lemon, halved

1 can (15 ounces/430 g) chickpeas, drained and rinsed

½ cup (120 ml) tahini

1 tablespoon white miso

1 teaspoon ground cumin

Optional garnishes: olive oil, za'atar, roasted chickpeas (see Notes), roasted garlic, fresh oregano

SET UP THE GRILL

Preheat a charcoal or gas grill to medium-high heat, and set it up with two zones: a hot side and cold (less hot) side, for direct and indirect cooking. (See method, page 15.) You want the temperature to hover around 400°F (205°C). (Alternatively, preheat the oven to 400°F/205°C.)

Slice ¼ to ½ inch (6 to 12 mm) off the top of the head of garlic to expose the individual cloves. Drizzle with a few teaspoons of olive oil and season with salt. Wrap the bulb tightly in foil and place it on the cooler side of grill (or in the oven), until the cloves are soft and have a golden, caramelized appearance, 40 to 45 minutes. Test after about 35 minutes, using your finger. While the garlic is finishing (even if you're doing it in the oven), set the lemon halves on greased grill grates and grill until charred and caramelized, 2 to 5 minutes.

Let the garlic cool briefly and then gently squeeze the roasted cloves out of the garlic bulb husk. Set aside 3 or 4 cloves for the hummus. (Save the remainder for another use; see Notes.)

In a blender or food processor, combine the chickpeas, tahini, miso, cumin, remaining ¼ cup (60 ml) olive oil, juice from one half of the grilled lemon, and the reserved grill-roasted garlic cloves and puree until very smooth. If the hummus is too thick, add cold water by the tablespoonful to thin it out, then season to taste with salt or more lemon juice.

Garnish with a drizzle of olive oil, za'atar, roasted chickpeas, roasted garlic, and fresh oregano, if using.

Notes: To roast chickpeas for garnish, toss with some olive oil, salt, and pepper and spread into an even layer on a sheet pan. Roast in a 425°F (220°C) oven for 20 to 30 minutes, shaking often for even cooking.

Store the roasted garlic, covered in olive oil, in an airtight container in the fridge for no more than 2 weeks.

SPINACH ARTICHOKE DIP BAKED ON A GRILL

SERVES 4

Add a Meyer lemon to just about anything and it instantly becomes not only a better version of itself—thanks to the sweet-tart nature of the citrus—but a California version of itself. The trees of this softer-skinned citrus grow particularly well in California, and the fruits are typically juicier than their Eureka counterparts, with more of an orange flavor than puckering lemon. It elevates this classic dip into something worthy of a fancy dinner party, especially when you let it bubble and broil on the grill. Serve it with chips, crackers, vegetables, or bread. Or just down it with a spoon when nobody's watching.

1 package (10 ounces/280 g) frozen chopped spinach, thawed and squeezed dry

1 jar (15 ounces/430 g) marinated artichoke hearts

8 ounces (225 g) cream cheese, at room temperature

½ cup (55 g) shredded Monterey Jack cheese

½ cup (50 g) grated Parmesan cheese

¼ cup (60 ml) mayonnaise

¼ cup (60 ml) sour cream

2 teaspoons grated Meyer lemon zest

1½ tablespoons Meyer lemon juice

2 teaspoons chopped fresh thyme

Kosher salt and freshly ground black pepper

SET UP THE GRILL

Preheat a charcoal or gas grill to medium-high heat, and set it up with two zones: a hot side and cold (less hot) side, for direct and indirect cooking. (See method, page 15.) You want the temperature to hover around 400°F (205°C).

In a large bowl, mix everything together until well combined. Season to taste with salt and pepper.

Spread the mixture in a 1-quart (1 L) cast-iron or other grill-safe dish and place on the cooler side of the grill. Close the grill and cook until bubbling and hot, 30 to 35 minutes.

Serve warm.

CHARRED GREEN ONION AND SALMON SPREAD

SERVES 8 AS AN APPETIZER

This throwback recipe is like a perfect bagel schmear, dip, and cracker spread in one. The grilled salmon makes all the difference here with its smoky notes. I use leftover grilled salmon or cook fresh before making the dip. Mixed with charred green onions, the whole thing gets rolled in a mixture of fresh dill, parsley, and everything bagel seasoning. It's a great make-ahead appetizer since it needs to firm up in the refrigerator and can be unmolded right before serving.

8 ounces (225 g) cream cheese, at room temperature

2 tablespoons sour cream

2 tablespoons mayonnaise

1 tablespoon Dijon mustard

Grated zest of 2 lemons

1 salmon fillet (4 ounces/115 g), grilled and flaked (about 1 cup/135 g)

4 grilled green onions, chopped

¼ cup (60 ml) everything bagel seasoning

½ bunch fresh dill, chopped

¼ bunch fresh parsley, chopped

Bagel chips, for serving

In a large bowl, mix together the cream cheese, sour cream, mayonnaise, mustard, half of the lemon zest, the flaked salmon, and green onions until well combined. Using plastic wrap to help shape the mixture, pull it all together into a ball shape and refrigerate until firm.

Once firm, spread the bagel seasoning, dill, parsley, and remaining lemon zest on a plate and mix together with your fingers to make a coating. Roll the cream cheese ball in the coating, pressing it into the sides as you go.

Serve with bagel chips.

QUICK FIRE

THERE'S A REASON THIS CHAPTER IS LONGER THAN ALL THE OTHERS, AND THAT'S BECAUSE I THINK IT'S WHERE YOU'LL SPEND THE MOST TIME. Consider this the weeknight dinner chapter, filled with an abundance of recipe inspiration for simpler, faster meals. There are other places in the book where you'll stoke wood chips in a smoker for hours on end, or even be compelled to fire up the grill on a weekend morning. But in this chapter, you'll find the best ways to cook all types of chicken, with essential tips and tricks to keep it from drying out on the grill. You'll cook shellfish in minutes, find family-favorite taco recipes, and get access to what I believe is the best smash burger around.

This is also the chapter where I'd encourage you to get creative. Like clams better than mussels but interested in the green curry? Switch them up. Make the piccata butter that goes with the Reverse-Seared Grilled Chicken (page 88) to serve on top of your Grilled Whole Trout (page 113)—it will totally play. Pair these recipes with your favorites from the Sides chapter for full dinner menus that take the guesswork out of planning.

GRILLED CHICKEN 101

SERVES 4

I used to think there was only one good way to cook boneless, skinless chicken breasts—that is, seared in a pan on the stove and finished in the oven, until just cooked through. But I think we might have developed an even better technique here, brining the white meat first (if you have time), then doing a direct-to-indirect jump on the grill, which will allow you to get both the grill marks and the juiciness. I sometimes like to make a bunch of these on the weekend and use in other dishes throughout the week—this chicken is great cold on a Caesar salad, chopped up for tacos or quesadillas, or used in a rice or noodle bowl with other accompaniments of your choice.

4 teaspoons kosher salt

1 teaspoon sugar

2 sprigs each rosemary, thyme, and sage

½ lemon, cut into slices

2 cloves garlic, smashed and peeled

1 teaspoon black peppercorns

1 teaspoon coriander seeds

4 boneless, skinless chicken breasts (about 6 to 8 ounces/170 to 225 g) each)

Extra-virgin olive oil

In a small pot, combine 1 quart (960 ml) water, salt, sugar, herb sprigs, lemon slices, garlic, peppercorns, and coriander seeds. Bring to a point just before a simmer, about 180°F (82°C). Do not boil. Let cool down completely.

Once cool, place the chicken into the brine and fully submerge. Let sit in the brine at room temperature for 2 to 3 hours. If longer, keep in the refrigerator, taking out to bring to room temperature before grilling.

SET UP THE GRILL

When ready to finish, preheat a charcoal or gas grill to medium-high heat, and set it up with two zones: a hot side and cold (less hot) side, for direct and indirect cooking. (See method, page 15.) You want the temperature to hover around 400°F (205°C).

Grease the grill grates with cooking spray.

Remove the chicken from the brine and pat dry on paper towels. Rub a touch of olive oil onto the breasts to prevent them from sticking to the grill.

Place the chicken breasts on the hot side of the grill for about 3 minutes, or until they have some nice color and grill marks. Flip over and repeat on the other side for about 3 minutes. This will give you all the color you want but not completely cook the chicken. Transfer from the hot side of the grill to the cooler side of the grill, close the lid, and cook until the chicken has reached an internal temperature of 155°F (86°C), 3 to 4 more minutes. Let rest 5 to 10 minutes before serving. By the time it rests, it will carryover cook and should settle around 160°F (71°C).

REVERSE-SEARED GRILLED CHICKEN BASE RECIPE

SERVES 4 TO 6

Grilling bone-in chicken pieces is much harder than it seems—usually you'll end up with a charred exterior and either a dry or undercooked interior, always seeming to miss that elusive perfect middle. This recipe was created to make it foolproof. The reverse-sear method means we first bake it low and slow, cooking it from the inside out, to prevent moisture loss. Baked with a quick dry brine that flavors as it cooks, the chicken gets most of the way there while the grill is warming up. Then it moves to the grill for the "reverse sear," where it gets that signature smokiness and crisp skin. Serve it plain or with any of the sauce options in the following pages.

1 whole chicken (3 to 4 pounds/1.4 to 1.8 kg), broken down into 10 pieces
Reverse-Sear Dry Brine (page 238)

SLOW-BAKE THE CHICKEN

Preheat the oven to 220°F (110°C)—be sure not to have it on the convection setting. Line a sheet pan with parchment paper.

In a large bowl, toss the chicken with the dry brine ingredients. Mix well until everything is coated.

Arrange the chicken on the lined pan. Transfer to the oven and bake until an instant-read thermometer inserted into the thickest part of the thigh reads 130°F (54°C), about 40 minutes. Remove from the oven to rest. At this point the chicken is partially cooked. You can place it in a zip-seal storage bag and store it for later use, or freeze until needed. If desired, you can even add a marinade or sauce and refrigerate to use within 24 hours.

SET UP THE GRILL

When ready to finish, preheat a charcoal or gas grill to medium-high heat, and set it up with two zones: a hot side and cold (less hot) side, for direct and indirect cooking. (See method, page 15.) You want the temperature to hover around 400°F (205°C).

REVERSE-SEAR THE CHICKEN

Place the chicken on the hot side of the grill. Rotate and flip every 5 minutes from the hot side to the cooler side to create an even sear on the chicken without burning it. Cook until a thermometer inserted into the thickest part of the thigh reads 155°F (68°C), about 25 minutes from cold or 12 minutes from room temperature.

Remove the chicken from the grill and let rest before serving.

REVERSE-SEARED GRILLED CHICKEN WITH PICCATA BUTTER

SERVES 4 TO 6

Reverse-Seared Grilled Chicken Base Recipe
(page 87)

For the piccata butter

1 stick (8 ounces/225 g) unsalted butter

¼ cup (60 ml) extra-virgin olive oil

2 cloves garlic, peeled

2 oil-packed anchovy fillets

1 teaspoon kosher salt

1½ tablespoons brined capers, drained

2 lemons, segmented (see Note) and diced

½ bunch fresh chives, minced

¼ bunch fresh parsley, minced

For garnish

Lemon wedges

Parsley leaves

Parmigiano-Reggiano cheese

Dry-brine, slow-bake, and reverse-sear the chicken as directed in the recipe.

MEANWHILE, MAKE THE PICCATA BUTTER

Set a small grill-safe pot with the butter and olive oil on the grill and cook until the butter begins to break and bubble.

While the butter and oil are heating, place the garlic, anchovies, and salt on a cutting board and roughly chop it all together. Once chopped up, use the edge of your knife to scrape the anchovy/garlic/salt mixture into a paste. Transfer to a small bowl and add the capers and lemon segments to it.

Once the oil and butter have heated, add the anchovy mixture to the pot and cook for 2 to 3 minutes to release all the flavors. Add the minced chives and parsley to the pot right before you serve it.

Place the chicken on a large platter and pour the piccata butter evenly over the top. Garnish with lemon wedges, parsley leaves, and Parmigiano-Reggiano cheese. Serve warm.

Note: To segment the lemon, slice off the peel and pith in sections, following the shape of the lemon. Starting at one segment of the lemon, cut toward the center along the membrane. Then slice along the adjacent membrane until the cuts meet in the middle and the segment is released. Transfer to a bowl and repeat with the remaining segments.

REVERSE-SEARED GRILLED CHICKEN WITH BARBECUE SAUCE

SERVES 4 TO 6

Reverse-Seared Grilled Chicken Base Recipe
  (page 87)
BBQ Sauce (page 238)
Fried pickles (optional; see Note)

Dry-brine and slow-bake the chicken as directed in the recipe.

While the chicken is slow-baking in the oven, make the BBQ sauce on the stovetop.

SET UP THE GRILL
Follow the directions for grilling the chicken, and baste it occasionally with the BBQ sauce as it cooks.

Serve hot with extra sauce on the side, topped with fried pickles if desired.

Note: To make the fried pickles, dip bread and butter or dill pickle slices into a dredge made from ¾ cup (95 g) flour, ¼ cup (55 g) polenta, 2 teaspoons kosher salt, 1 teaspoon onion powder, and 1 teaspoon garlic powder mixed together. Shallow-fry the pickles until the coating is crisp and golden. Drain on paper towels.

REVERSE-SEARED GRILLED HULI HULI CHICKEN

SERVES 4 TO 6

Reverse-Seared Grilled Chicken Base Recipe
(page 87)

For the huli huli sauce

½ cup (120 ml) ketchup
½ cup (120 ml) pineapple juice
⅓ cup (75 g) brown sugar
¼ cup (60 ml) soy sauce
2 tablespoons rice vinegar
1 tablespoon grated fresh ginger
1 tablespoon grated green onions
1 tablespoon grated garlic
1½ tablespoons sambal oelek

For the accompaniments

1 pound (455 g) sweet Italian red peppers
1 pineapple, peeled, cored, and cut into
 ½-inch (1.3 cm) rings
Extra-virgin olive oil, for brushing
Kosher salt and freshly ground black pepper
Sliced green onions, for garnish
Sesame seeds, for garnish

Dry-brine and slow-bake the chicken as directed in the recipe.

MEANWHILE, MAKE THE HULI HULI SAUCE

While the chicken is baking in the oven, make the sauce on the stovetop. In a small pot, combine all the sauce ingredients and whisk together well. Bring to a quick simmer over medium heat to melt the sugar and let the ginger, green onions, and garlic extract a bit. Let cool before using.

SET UP THE GRILL

Follow the directions for grilling the chicken, and baste it occasionally with the huli huli sauce as it cooks.

When the chicken is 10 to 12 minutes from being done (or at the same time if you started with chicken at room temp), brush the red peppers and pineapple with a little bit of olive oil and season lightly with salt and pepper. Place on the hot side of the grill. Cook the pineapple for 8 to 10 minutes, flipping once halfway through cooking. Keep the peppers on a few minutes longer until the chicken is done, turning often, until slightly charred and softened.

Plate the chicken with the peppers and pineapple. Garnish with thinly sliced green onions and sesame seeds. Serve immediately.

REVERSE-SEARED POLLO ASADO

SERVES 4 TO 6

Reverse-Seared Grilled Chicken Base Recipe
   (page 87)

For the pollo asado marinade

¼ cup (60 ml) extra-virgin olive oil

¼ cup (60 ml) fresh lime juice

¼ cup (55 g) minced jalapeños

1 teaspoon ground coriander

1 teaspoon ground cumin

For serving

Corn tortillas

Pickled Red Onions (recipe follows)

Cotija cheese

Fresh cilantro

Thinly sliced radishes

Lime wedges

Pico de Gallo (optional; page 98)

Dry-brine and slow-bake the chicken as directed in the recipe.

MEANWHILE, MAKE THE POLLO ASADO MARINADE
In a large bowl, stir together the olive oil, lime juice, jalapeños, coriander, and cumin. Toss with the chicken and marinate in the refrigerator for at least 30 minutes, up to overnight.

SET UP THE GRILL
When ready to finish, preheat a charcoal or gas grill to medium-high heat, and set it up with two zones: a hot side and cold (less hot) side, for direct and indirect cooking. (See method, page 15.) You want the temperature to hover around 400°F (205°C). Place a cast-iron flattop griddle on the grates while the grill is heating. We do this on a griddle as opposed to the grates so that the chicken cooks in the juices of the marinade without falling through.

When the griddle is hot, place the chicken on top. Start on the hot side of the grill to sear the chicken, then move the griddle to the cooler side after a few minutes. Cook until a thermometer inserted into the thickest part of the thigh reads 155°F (68°C), about 25 minutes if cooking from cold or 12 minutes if cooking from room temperature. Baste the chicken occasionally with the juices running off the chicken as it cooks.

Serve with the tortillas, pickled red onions, Cotija cheese, fresh cilantro, radishes, lime, and pico de gallo, if using.

PICKLED RED ONIONS

MAKES 1½ CUPS (360 ML)

Keep these in the fridge to garnish Mexican dishes like the Reverse-Seared Pollo Asado (recipe above), Halibut Fish Tacos (page 96), or Chicken Tender Tacos (page 98) or simply to add to sandwiches or salads. They add just the right amount of punch and crunch to everything.

1 cup (240 ml) red wine vinegar

¼ cup (50 g) granulated sugar

Kosher salt and freshly ground black pepper

1 red onion, sliced

4 ice cubes (120 g)

In a small saucepan, combine ½ cup (120 ml) water, the vinegar, sugar, and salt and pepper to taste. Bring to a boil. Place the sliced onions in a small sealable, heatproof container. Pour the hot solution over the onions and stir. Add the ice cubes to the top of the onions to weight them down and cool them. Cover the container and place in the refrigerator for at least 1 hour or until cool.

HALIBUT FISH TACOS

SERVES 4 TO 6

For a few seasons of *The Great Food Truck Race*, I filmed a digital companion series called *The Extra Mile*, where I would check out local restaurants on the road during my downtime. It was a great way to sample regional cuisine. On one trip to San Diego, I did my fair share of fish taco sampling, and though I always love the Baja crispy-style fish, there were some versions of healthier grilled fish tacos that I often re-create at home. Everyone loves this summertime staple, which is a great add to the weekly rotation.

For the pink chile mayo

½ cup (120 ml) mayonnaise

2 tablespoons sriracha

½ teaspoon ground cumin

For the fish

2 tablespoons extra-virgin olive oil

2 to 3 pieces skin-on halibut fillet (8 ounces/ 225 g each)

Kosher salt and freshly ground black pepper

For the tacos

8 (6-inch/15 cm) corn tortillas

½ recipe Pico de Gallo (page 98)

Fresh cilantro leaves, for garnish

Chopped green onion, for garnish

Lime wedges, for squeezing

MAKE THE PINK CHILE MAYO

In a small bowl, combine the mayonnaise, sriracha, and cumin and mix until fully incorporated. Set aside.

SET UP THE GRILL

Preheat a charcoal or gas grill to medium-high heat with a target temperature of 400°F (205°C). Place a large cast-iron flattop griddle or skillet with a couple tablespoons of olive oil onto the hot grill to heat up.

GRILL THE FISH

Once the griddle and oil are hot, place the fish skin-side down onto the griddle and cook until the skin is crispy and browned, 5 to 6 minutes. Season the flesh side of the fish with salt and pepper and flip over to sear for about 2 minutes or so to finish cooking and brown the flesh.

ASSEMBLE THE TACOS

Place the tortillas straight on the grill grates for 15 to 20 seconds per side to heat up and toast. If you are plating them individually, use a fork to flake the flesh of the fish away from the skin. Discard the skin. Smear some of the chile mayo inside one of the tortillas. Fill with fish and top with the pico de gallo. Garnish with cilantro and green onions and serve with a lime wedge for squeezing. Repeat with remaining tacos. Alternatively, serve everything family-style for people to assemble their own tacos.

KIDS' CHICKEN TENDER TACOS

SERVES 4 TO 6

I love these chicken tacos for their weeknight ease—whole tenders go on the grill and are the perfect amount to use: one per taco. This meal is about as kid-friendly as it gets, and you don't need to go overboard with the toppings—think of the below as suggestions.

For the marinated chicken

¼ cup (60 ml) extra-virgin olive oil

¼ cup (60 ml) fresh lime juice

¼ cup (55 g) minced jalapeños

1 teaspoon ground coriander

1 teaspoon ground cumin

12 chicken tenders (about 1½ pounds/680 g)

Kosher salt and freshly ground black pepper

For the avocado mash

2 avocados, halved and pitted

¾ cup (340 g) Pico de Gallo (recipe follows)

Kosher salt

For the tacos

12 corn tortillas

Sliced radishes

Fresh cilantro

Pickled Red Onions (page 95)

Cotija cheese

3 limes, halved and grilled (see Grilled Citrus Garnish, page 21)

MARINATE THE CHICKEN

In a bowl, stir together the olive oil, lime juice, jalapeños, coriander, and cumin. Toss the chicken to coat and let marinate while you prepare everything else and preheat the grill. You can leave the chicken in the marinade up to 2 hours but no longer, as the acid from the limes will start to "cook" the chicken.

SET UP THE GRILL

Preheat a charcoal or gas grill to medium-high heat with a target temperature of 400°F (205°C).

GRILL THE CHICKEN

Remove the chicken tenders from the marinade, shake off excess, and season with salt and pepper. Place directly on the grates and grill for 7 to 8 minutes, turning once, or until cooked through.

MAKE THE AVOCADO MASH

Scoop the avocado flesh into a bowl and mash with a fork. Mix in the pico de gallo. Season with salt.

ASSEMBLE THE TACOS

In each tortilla, spread some of the avocado mash. Top each with 1 chicken tender and garnish with any combination of radishes, cilantro, pickled red onions, and Cotija cheese you desire. Squeeze grilled lime juice over everything and serve immediately.

PICO DE GALLO

MAKES 2 CUPS (475 ML)

Serve the pico with chips or use for the Halibut Fish Tacos (page 96) or as one of the garnishes for the Reverse-Seared Pollo Asado (page 95).

16 ounces (455 g) cherry tomatoes, quartered

1 small yellow onion, diced small

2 jalapeños, thinly sliced

¼ cup (60 ml) lime juice (about 4 limes)

⅓ cup (15 g) chopped fresh cilantro

2 teaspoons kosher salt

In a bowl, combine the tomatoes, onion, jalapeños, lime juice, and cilantro. Season with the salt. Mix until combined. If not using right away, store in the refrigerator.

DOUBLE-BACON SMASH BURGERS

SERVES 4

This homemade "double-double" rivals the In-N-Out version. It's all the things: ultrathin smashed patties, a "secret sauce" flavored with pepperoncini (make the full recipe to have some extra for a rainy day), sweet caramelized onions, and thick-sliced bacon. Hot tip: If you can find deli lids (like the type that come with takeout), they make perfectly shaped thin patty molds. Cook the patties on a cast-iron flattop griddle set on top of the grill, which is a great way to get the smokiness you're looking for without things sticking or falling apart—especially important when dealing with such thin burgers.

For the secret sauce

1 cup (240 ml) mayonnaise

⅓ cup (75 ml) yellow mustard

¼ cup (60 ml) ketchup

1 teaspoon garlic salt

2 tablespoons chopped pepperoncini

2 tablespoons sweet relish

For the burgers

1 pound (455 g) ground beef

1 tablespoon extra-virgin olive oil

1 yellow onion, diced

Kosher salt

4 slices thick-cut bacon, halved

4 burger buns, such as potato, King's
   Hawaiian, or brioche

Oil, for the buns

Freshly ground black pepper

8 slices American cheese

½ head iceberg lettuce, shaved or thinly
   sliced

MAKE THE SECRET SAUCE

In a small bowl, stir together all the ingredients. Set aside.

PREP THE BURGER PATTIES

Divide the hamburger meat into 8 equal portions (2 ounces/57 g each) and form into balls. Place each ball between two deli lids or between two sheets of plastic wrap. Smash to make a nice even patty that is ½ to 1 inch (1.3 to 2.5 cm) wider than your bun. Place the patties on parchment paper and wrap in plastic wrap. Set these in the fridge for about 10 minutes before cooking. This process will not only help shape the burger patties but also allow them to rest in that shape and result in less shrinkage when cooking. The plastic wrap will help keep the meat from oxidizing while resting.

Meanwhile, in a medium sauté pan, heat the oil over medium heat. Once the oil begins to shimmer and smoke, add the diced onion and season with salt. Sauté until the onions begin to slightly darken and caramelize, 4 to 5 minutes. Scrape the onions into a small bowl and set aside.

Wipe out the pan. Place the bacon in the same pan, set over medium heat, and cook until it begins to brown, 2 to 3 minutes per side. You do not want this crispy. Once finished, place the bacon on a tray lined with paper towels and set aside.

SET UP THE GRILL

Preheat a charcoal or gas grill to medium-high heat with a target temperature of 400°F (205°C). Place a large cast-iron flattop griddle or skillet onto the grates to heat up. Spray with cooking spray or rub with oil. Split the buns in half and spray or brush the cut sides with oil. While the griddle is heating up, place the buns cut side down onto the griddle to toast until dark golden brown, 1 to 2 minutes. Once toasted, set the buns aside.

COOK THE BURGERS

Season 2 patties with salt and pepper and place them on the griddle along with 2 slices of bacon. Sear the beef patties for about 1 minute and flip over. As soon as you flip the patties over, place a slice of American cheese on each patty to melt. Once the cheese has melted, stack the patties on top of one another and place the 2 strips of bacon on top. Repeat with remaining burgers.

Place some of the shredded lettuce on top of the bottom half of the bun. Then place the stacked cheeseburgers and bacon on top of the lettuce. Add a spoonful of the cooked onions to the top of the bacon. Add a spoonful of the secret sauce to the top side of the bun and spread out evenly. Place the tops of the buns onto the burgers. Serve warm.

GRILLED CHICKEN PAILLARDS WITH FENNEL, ARUGULA, AND GRAPEFRUIT SALAD

SERVES 3 OR 4

This is one of those insanely simple recipes that's as good for Tuesday solo dining as it is for a dinner party—it takes longer to heat up the grill than it does to cook the chicken, and the salad can be prepped ahead of time as well (add the greens at the last minute). The salad on top can really be anything—arugula and parm, Italian Chopped Salad (page 65), or any seasonal combination of greens and vegetables. We debated the inclusion of both tomatoes and grapefruit here, as it straddles the seasons a bit. In the end, however, we loved the acidic pop of both unexpected flavors together with briny olives and feta.

2 boneless, skinless chicken breasts
Kosher salt and freshly ground black pepper

For the salad

1 fennel bulb, shaved
1 grapefruit, segmented (see Note, page 88)
½ cup (75 g) crumbled feta cheese
¼ cup (55 g) sliced green olives
1 cup (75 g) assorted leafy greens
½ cup (115 g) halved cherry tomatoes
2 tablespoons minced fresh chives
¼ cup (60 ml) extra-virgin olive oil
Kosher salt

Cut each chicken breast horizontally into 2 thin cutlets. With a meat pounder or small skillet, pound the cutlets to a ½-inch (1.3 cm) thickness.

SET UP THE GRILL

Preheat a charcoal or gas grill to medium-high heat with a target temperature of 400°F (205°C). Season the chicken with salt and pepper on both sides.

MAKE THE SALAD

In a bowl, toss together the fennel, grapefruit, feta, olives, leafy greens, and tomatoes. Mix the chives and olive oil together in a separate bowl but do not toss with the salad yet. Set both aside.

GRILL THE CHICKEN

When the grill is hot, place the chicken directly onto the grates. Grill until cooked through with visible grill marks, 2 to 3 minutes per side.

Remove the chicken and transfer to plates or a platter. Brush the top of the chicken with the chive oil. Toss the rest of the chive oil with the salad and season to taste with a little bit of salt (you won't need much because of the olives and feta). Top the chicken with the salad and serve immediately.

GRILLED SALMON NIÇOISE

SERVES 3 OR 4

This is what we like to call "stab and grab," and we're convinced that it is most people's favorite way to eat. No fussy, composed lettuce salad here; this grilled salad is less of a traditional Niçoise and more a beautiful platter of salmon and vegetables—and a great way to stretch the expensive fish. Plated, it looks a little edgier than what you might normally serve as a quick weeknight dinner, but with everything you want in one meal.

For the vegetables

Kosher salt

8 ounces (225 g) marble potatoes

4 ounces (115 g) green beans, cleaned

3 to 4 ounces (85 to 115 g) Kalamata olives, finely minced

¼ cup (60 ml) extra-virgin olive oil

For the salmon

2 to 3 tablespoons extra-virgin olive oil

12 ounces (340 g) skin-on salmon

Kosher salt and freshly ground black pepper

For the salad

1 cup Pistou Dressing (page 105)

2 radishes, shaved thin, or 4 radishes, quartered

2 soft-boiled eggs (see Note), quartered

2 ounces (58 g) leafy greens, such as arugula, baby spinach, baby kale, pea shoots

Lemon wedges, for squeezing

SET UP THE GRILL

Preheat a charcoal or gas grill to high heat with a target temperature of 500°F (260°C). Place a cast-iron skillet or cast-iron flattop griddle on the grates.

PREPARE THE VEGETABLES

Bring a large pot of salted water to a simmer. Place the potatoes into the pot and cook until they are tender enough to be smashed by pressing on them, about 10 minutes. With 1 minute left to cook the potatoes, throw the green beans into the pot and finish cooking together. Pour the pot out into a colander and rinse the potatoes and green beans with cold water to stop the cooking process (or place them into a bowl of ice water). Once the potatoes and green beans are cooled, set them aside. In a small bowl, mix the minced olives with the olive oil and set aside.

GRILL THE SALMON

Add some olive oil to the skillet or rub onto the griddle. Season the fish generously with salt and pepper. Once the oil starts to shimmer and smoke, place the salmon, flesh-side down, onto the griddle or pan. Cook until the flesh side is beginning to brown and crisp, 3 to 4 minutes. Gently flip the fish over and finish cooking for 1 to 2 minutes more, depending on your desired doneness. Remove the salmon from the pan and rest on a plate or tray lined with paper towels to soak up any excess oil.

ASSEMBLE THE SALAD

Place a large spoonful of the pistou down onto the plate in the shape of a large ring or circle. Do the same with the Kalamata/oil mixture. Flake the salmon and arrange the fish and the other ingredients scattered around the plate. Feel free to drizzle a little olive oil over the top, or a squeeze of lemon. Serve immediately.

Note: To make soft-boiled eggs, set up a bowl of ice and water. Bring a pot of water to a simmer and gently drop in the eggs. Cook for 6 to 9 minutes, depending on how soft you want the yolks. Submerge in the ice bath to stop cooking.

PISTOU DRESSING

MAKES 2 CUPS (475 ML)

Use this dressing for salads or to top grilled meat or fish. To make the garlic a little less spicy in the dressing, it gets blanched for a few minutes to take the edge off.

Kosher salt
½ cup (115 g) peeled garlic cloves
1 bunch fresh parsley, roughly chopped
¼ bunch fresh basil, leaves and stems
Grated zest of 1 lemon
1¼ cups (300 ml) extra-virgin olive oil

Set up a bowl of ice and water. Bring a small pot of salted water to a boil. Place the whole cloves of garlic into the boiling water and blanch for 2 minutes. Scoop the garlic into the ice bath to stop the cooking and completely cool. Drain well.

In a blender, combine the blanched garlic, parsley, basil, lemon zest, 1 teaspoon kosher salt, and the oil and puree on high speed until smooth, about 30 seconds.

GRILLED SAUSAGE SANDWICHES WITH GIARDINIERA AND APPLE MUSTARD

SERVES 6 TO 8

Rather than include a simple hot dog recipe, I opted for these leveled-up grilled sausage sandwiches. The technique itself is pretty simple—charred on the hot side of the grill and finished over indirect heat—but what makes these so special are the condiments on top. Forget ketchup and French's, here we've got sweet apple mustard and tart, crisp giardiniera, a traditional Italian pickled topping that is great with any grilled meat. You'll want to make that ahead of time, as it needs to marinate for a while—the longer it sits, the better. Prep the apple mustard early, too, in order to make this dish ready for quick assembly at dinnertime.

For the giardiniera

1 tablespoon coriander seeds

1 tablespoons fennel seeds

5 stalks celery, thinly sliced

1 fennel bulb, thinly sliced

1 small yellow onion, thinly sliced

2 red Fresno chiles, sliced

1 teaspoon chile flakes

1 teaspoon celery seeds

1½ cups (360 ml) distilled white vinegar

1 tablespoon kosher salt

2 teaspoons sugar

For the sausages

8 hot or sweet Italian sausages, uncooked

8 hot dog or long sandwich buns

Apple Mustard (page 243)

MAKE THE GIARDINIERA

In a small dry skillet, toast the coriander and fennel seeds over medium-low heat until fragrant. Transfer to a large bowl and add the sliced celery, sliced fennel, onion, chiles, chile flakes, celery seeds, vinegar, salt, sugar, ½ cup (120 ml) water, and 1½ cups (340 g) ice. Place in the refrigerator and marinate for at least 3 hours, but the longer the better.

SET UP THE GRILL

Preheat a charcoal or gas grill to medium-high heat, and set it up with two zones: a hot side and cold (less hot) side, for direct and indirect cooking. (See method, page 15.) You want the temperature to hover around 400°F (205°C).

GRILL THE SAUSAGES

Poke a few holes in each sausage to let steam escape. Put the sausages on the grill grate over the hot side of the grill. Cook, turning once or twice, until the outside is slightly charred, 3 to 4 minutes total. Move to the cooler side of the grill and close the lid. Continue to cook until a thermometer inserted into the middle reads 145°F (62°C), 8 to 10 minutes.

To assemble, place one sausage in each bun. Top with giardiniera and apple mustard and serve hot.

WILLIAMS-SONOMA

PORK NOODLE BOWLS

SERVES 4

This is one of those recipes where just making the pork to serve with a salad or side dish would be great as is, so if that's all you have time and energy for, stop there. But if you're willing to take it a step further, these vermicelli bowls are beautiful, and filled with a great balance of sweet, spicy, crunchy, and herbal elements. Most of it will come together while the pork cooks, and you can either preassemble the bowls before serving or let people DIY at the table. You can find both the vermicelli noodles and the sambal oelek—an Indonesian spice paste made from ground chiles, vinegar, and salt—in the Asian section of the grocery store.

For the marinated pork

3 cloves garlic, peeled

1 knob ginger, peeled and roughly chopped

½ stalk lemongrass, cleaned and roughly
    chopped

Grated zest of 1 lime

2 tablespoons fish sauce

1 tablespoon sambal oelek

1 tablespoon hoisin sauce

1 tablespoon reduced-sodium soy sauce

1 teaspoon cumin seeds

1 teaspoon coriander seeds

1 teaspoon freshly ground black pepper

1 teaspoon kosher salt

1 pound (445 g) pork tenderloin

For the nuoc cham sauce

¼ cup (50 g) sugar

¼ cup (60 ml) fish sauce

1 clove garlic, grated

1 teaspoon sambal oelek

Juice of 2 limes

For the pork bowls

1 (8 ounce/225 g) package rice noodles,
    soaked in warm water for 10 to 20 minutes
    or until soft

1 large carrot, cut into matchsticks

1 daikon radish, cut into matchsticks

1 to 2 jalapeños, thinly sliced

1 bunch green onions, thinly sliced

2 tablespoons white sesame seeds, toasted

Fresh mint sprigs, for garnish

2 limes, cut into wedges, for garnish

½ cup (75 g) roasted peanuts, chopped, for
    garnish

MARINATE THE PORK

In a high-powered blender or food processor, combine the garlic, ginger, lemongrass, ¼ cup (60 ml) water, lime zest, fish sauce, sambal, hoisin, soy sauce, and all the spices and blend for 30 to 45 seconds to break up all the garlic, ginger, seeds, and lemongrass.

Place the pork in a zip-seal storage bag and pour the marinade over the top. Let sit for a few hours in the refrigerator, or up to overnight.

MAKE THE NUOC CHAM SAUCE

In a small pot, combine ½ cup (120 ml) water and the sugar and stir over medium heat until the sugar dissolves. Add the fish sauce, garlic, sambal, and lime juice and taste for seasoning, adding more lime juice if necessary. Set aside in the refrigerator.

SET UP THE GRILL

Preheat a charcoal or gas grill to medium-high heat, and set it up with two zones: a hot side and cold (less hot) side, for direct and indirect cooking. (See method, page 15.) You want the temperature to hover around 400°F (205°C).

Remove the tenderloin from the marinade. Place the pork on a paper towel and pat dry. Pour the marinade from the bag into a pot on the stovetop and bring to a simmer over medium heat. Simmer for 4 to 5 minutes. This will cook the raw ingredients of the marinade and allow it to thicken into a sauce that will be brushed over the pork as it cooks.

GRILL THE PORK

Place the pork onto the hot side of the grill and cook for 3 to 4 minutes. Flip over and cook until it gets a nice char and some deep brown coloring, another 3 to 4 minutes. Move to the cooler side of the grill and baste with the marinade. Close the lid and cook until the pork reaches an internal temperature of 130° to 135°F (54° to 57°C), another 5 to 6 minutes. Remove the tenderloin from the grill and let rest on a tray for 8 to 10 minutes before slicing.

BUILD THE PORK BOWLS

Divide the noodles among four bowls. Mix the carrot and the daikon together and place in a section of each bowl on top of the noodles. Place sliced jalapeños next to that, followed by the sliced green onions. Brush the tenderloin with a little more of the cooked marinade and slice. Place a few slices in each bowl and top with some sesame seeds. Garnish the bowl with a few sprigs of mint, lime wedges, and some crushed peanuts. Drizzle with the nuoc cham sauce or serve on the side.

GRILLED CLAMS CASINO

SERVES 4

This is one of my Food Network classics from a show I used to host called *Tyler's Ultimate*, where I would find the best version of a particular dish, from chicken cacciatore to cioppino. The inspiration for this recipe actually came from one for oysters casino, but the sauce was really the best part. Here, I pair the pepper, herb, and bacon-studded butter with briny clams for the grill, and the result, in my opinion, is still pretty ultimate. Make sure you have some crusty bread on hand to mop up any extra sauce.

For the casino butter

1 stick (4 ounces/115 g) unsalted butter, at room temperature

2 cloves garlic, minced

¼ cup (35 g) roughly chopped shallots

¼ cup (35 g) roughly chopped red bell pepper

¼ cup (25 g) roughly chopped celery

2 teaspoons grated lemon zest

2 teaspoons fresh lemon juice

2 sprigs fresh oregano, leaves picked

2 sprigs fresh thyme, leaves picked

¼ teaspoon chile flakes

Kosher salt and freshly ground black pepper

For cooking and serving

4 slices bacon, cooked but not crisp, cut into small strips

2 pounds (910 g) Manila clams

1 orange, halved and grilled (see Grilled Citrus Garnish, page 21)

¼ bunch flat-leaf parsley, finely chopped, for garnish

Crusty bread, for serving

SET UP THE GRILL

Preheat a charcoal or gas grill to medium-high heat, and set it up with two zones: a hot side and cold (less hot) side, for direct and indirect cooking. (See method, page 15.) You want the temperature to hover around 400°F (205°C).

In a food processor, combine the butter, garlic, shallots, bell pepper, celery, lemon zest, lemon juice, oregano, thyme, and chile flakes and pulse until well combined, but still with texture. Season with salt and pepper to taste. Set the casino butter aside.

TO COOK

Once the grill is hot, create a "medium" zone by either adjusting the gas temperature or moving some of the charcoal from the hot side to the cooler side. Place a cast-iron or other grill-safe gratin or casserole dish on top of the grates on the medium zone. Add the casino butter and bacon to the dish and let the butter melt. Stir in the clams and cook, stirring occasionally, until they all open, 5 to 10 minutes, spooning and basting the sauce over the clams as they cook.

TO SERVE

Squeeze the grilled oranges over the clams and garnish with parsley. Serve with crusty bread for sopping up the sauce.

GRILLED WHOLE TROUT WITH GREEN BEANS AMANDINE

SERVES 4

A metal cooling rack is one of the newest accessories I've turned to while I grill—it's multifunctional because not only can you use it to transport food from the kitchen to the grill, but you can put the whole thing, ingredients and all, straight on the grates to get one step closer to the fire without something like this delicate fish sticking. Plus, it makes a pretty grid pattern on the food sitting on top. These green beans make a fantastic side dish for anything, but we love it with this lemon-and-thyme-scented whole trout. Ask your fishmonger to butterfly the fish if it's not displayed that way.

For the green beans

Kosher salt

1 pound (455 g) green beans

6 tablespoons (90 g) unsalted butter

2 shallots, finely minced

3 cloves garlic, minced

¾ cup (85 g) slivered almonds, toasted

Freshly ground black pepper

For the fish

Oil for the grill

3 whole trout, butterflied

2 tablespoons extra-virgin olive oil

Kosher salt and freshly ground black pepper

1 lemon, halved

1 bunch fresh thyme

Kosher salt and freshly ground black pepper

COOK THE GREEN BEANS

Set up a bowl of ice and water. Bring a large pot of salted water to a boil. Add the green beans and blanch until crisp-tender, about 3 minutes. Drain and place in the ice bath to stop cooking. Dry and set aside.

In a small pan, melt the butter set over medium-low heat. Cook, stirring occasionally, until the butter turns brown and nutty, taking care not to burn. Transfer the browned butter immediately to a large bowl and toss with the green beans, shallots, garlic, and almonds. Season to taste with salt and pepper.

SET UP THE GRILL

While the beans are cooking, preheat a charcoal or gas grill to medium-high heat with a target temperature of 400°F (205°C). Grease a metal cooling rack or fish basket with oil.

GRILL THE FISH

Rub the trout all over with the olive oil and season to taste with salt and pepper. Place flesh-side down on the greased cooling rack or basket, along with a halved lemon (flesh-side down). Drape sprigs of fresh thyme over the fish. Place the cooling rack straight onto the grill and cook, flipping carefully once, until cooked through, 5 to 6 minutes.

Squeeze the grilled lemon over the fish and garnish with the thyme. Serve with the green beans amandine.

GRILLED GREEN CURRY MUSSELS

SERVES 4

These mussels are hard not to eat straight off the grill. Cooked until they crack open in a grill basket with some stalks of fresh lemongrass and bright lime halves, they're delicious as is. But you'd be missing out if you didn't take it a step further by finishing them in a bright green curry sauce, which brings some fragrant Thai notes into the dish. It's a little unexpected, which is often the best way to go when bringing shellfish to the grill.

For the green curry sauce

3 stalks lemongrass, bottom 5 inches only

2 jalapeños, seeded and roughly chopped

1 shallot, roughly chopped

2-inch (5 cm) knob fresh ginger, peeled and roughly chopped

3 cloves garlic, smashed and peeled

2 makrut lime leaves

Grated zest and juice of 1 lime

½ cup (15 g) packed fresh cilantro leaves and tender stems

¼ cup (60 ml) coconut milk

½ teaspoon fish sauce

½ teaspoon ground coriander

½ teaspoon ground cumin

½ teaspoon ground turmeric

½ teaspoon kosher salt

¼ teaspoon ground white pepper

For the mussels

2 pounds (910 g) mussels, cleaned

3 whole stalks lemongrass, for the grill

2 limes, halved, for garnish

Fresh cilantro, for garnish

MAKE THE GREEN CURRY SAUCE

Discard the outer leaves of the lemongrass and slice the tender cores. In a food processor or blender, combine the lemongrass, jalapeños, shallot, ginger, garlic, lime leaves, lime zest, lime juice, cilantro, coconut milk, fish sauce, coriander, cumin, turmeric, salt, and white pepper and blend to a puree. Add 2 to 3 tablespoons water as needed to thin. This can be done up to a day in advance and refrigerated until needed.

SET UP THE GRILL

Preheat a charcoal or gas grill to medium-high heat with a target temperature of 400°F (205°C).

GRILL THE MUSSELS

Place the mussels inside a grill basket and scatter the lemongrass stalks and lime halves in and around the mussels. Close the basket. Place on the grill and cook, flipping every few minutes, until the shells open. Spoon sauce over the mussels and toss to coat. Cook for a couple more minutes.

Transfer the mussels to a serving dish and garnish with grilled lime and cilantro sprigs.

TERIYAKI CEDAR PLANK SALMON

SERVES 4

This is another one of those fun accessory recipes—salmon cooked on a plank made of cedar wood. Not only does it give the salmon a bit of smoky wood flavor, but it also slows down the cooking time and allows the flavors to really come together, which is great with a fish like salmon. You can purchase the planks on Amazon or from any well-stocked kitchen store. Alternatively, this will be equally delicious cooked on a cast-iron flattop griddle. At our house, I love serving this dish with the Broccoli Rice Pilaf (page 199) for a full dinner.

1 to 2 cedar planks (see Note)

4 salmon fillets (6 ounces/170 g each)

Kosher salt and freshly ground black pepper

1 tablespoon extra-virgin olive oil

Teriyaki Sauce (page 241)

Chopped green onions, for garnish

Toasted sesame seeds, for garnish

Fresh cilantro sprigs, for garnish

SET UP THE GRILL

Preheat a charcoal or gas grill to medium-high heat with a target temperature of 400°F (205°C).

Once hot, add the plank(s) and heat until they smoke and crackle a bit.

Season the salmon with salt and pepper and rub with the olive oil. Place directly on the cedar planks and close the lid of the grill. Cook until the fish flakes, about 20 minutes, basting with the teriyaki sauce every few minutes.

Garnish with chopped green onions, sesame seeds, and sprigs of cilantro. Serve with extra teriyaki sauce on the side.

Note: Cedar planks come in different sizes. Get the number you need to hold the salmon fillets. Submerge the cedar plank(s) in a container of water and soak for 2 hours.

BBQ TURKEY MEATBALL SLIDERS

SERVES 6

During a trip to Italy years ago, I learned one of my favorite tricks for
making a perfectly tender meatball with layers of flavor. While most recipes
in America call for minced raw garlic and onions, there I was instructed to
sauté them first, creating a deeper, caramelized base to add to the meat. Now
that's the foundation of every meatball or meatloaf recipe I make, whether
I'm doing a traditional Italian version in my oven or these sweet and savory
turkey meatballs for the grill. These would be delicious just on their own,
but here we like to serve them tucked into King's Hawaiian rolls as sliders
with a creamy cabbage slaw.

½ cup (40 g) panko bread crumbs

½ cup (120 ml) whole milk

2 tablespoons extra-virgin olive oil, plus more for cooking meatballs

½ yellow onion, diced

3 cloves garlic, sliced

3 slices bacon, diced

½ teaspoon chile flakes

1 pound (455 g) ground turkey

¼ cup (25 g) grated Parmesan cheese

½ bunch fresh parsley, leaves only, chopped

½ tablespoon kosher salt

½ teaspoon freshly ground black pepper

1 cup (240 ml) BBQ Sauce (page 238)

For the slaw

¼ cup sour cream

¼ cup mayonnaise

½ teaspoon onion powder

½ teaspoon garlic powder

1 tablespoon red wine vinegar

½ head red cabbage, shaved

1 bunch green onions, sliced

1 medium carrot, shaved

Kosher salt and freshly ground black pepper

12 King's Hawaiian Rolls

In a small bowl, stir together the panko and milk and set aside for at least 10 minutes so the panko can fully soak up all the milk.

In a small sauté pan, heat the olive oil over medium heat until the oil begins to shimmer and smoke. Add the onion, garlic, bacon, and chile flakes and cook, stirring occasionally, until the onions have fully softened and the bacon fat is rendered, about 10 minutes. Remove the pan from the heat and set aside to cool slightly before adding it to the meat.

In a large bowl, combine the ground turkey, Parmesan, parsley, salt, pepper, milk-soaked panko, and cooled bacon-onion mixture. Mix well until everything is evenly incorporated.

SET UP THE GRILL

Preheat a charcoal or gas grill to medium-high heat, and set it up with two zones: a hot side and cold (less hot) side, for direct and indirect cooking. (See method, page 15.) You want the temperature to hover around 400°F (205°C). While the grill is heating up, place a large cast-iron skillet on the hot side of the grill.

Using a large ice cream scoop, portion out and roll 12 meatballs. Add some oil to the skillet on the grill. When very hot and starting to shimmer, add the meatballs and cook, turning the meatballs, until the edges are browned, 3 to 4 minutes. Move the whole pan to the cooler side of the grill and close the lid. Continue to cook, basting often with the BBQ sauce, until the meatballs reach an internal temperature of 155°F (68°C), 10 to 12 minutes. Give them a final glaze and set aside.

MAKE THE SLAW

While the meatballs are cooking, combine the sour cream, mayonnaise, onion powder, garlic powder, and red wine vinegar in a bowl and mix well.

Place the shaved cabbage, sliced green onions, and shaved carrot into the bowl with the cream mixture and dress well. Season with salt and pepper to taste.

MAKE THE SLIDERS

Place a bit of the slaw on the bottom half of a King's Hawaiian roll. Place a meatball coated in BBQ sauce over the top of it and top it off with the top half of the roll. Serve warm and enjoy.

BEEF KOFTA WITH GRILLED EGGPLANT

SERVES 4 TO 6

I'm a fan of meatballs in all forms, and when it comes to Middle Eastern cuisine, that means kofta. Flavored with warm spices, these football-shaped cylinders are threaded onto skewers to become the anchor of a healthier meal that includes dips and spreads, side salads, and homemade pita bread. The kofta can be made ahead of time and either refrigerated or frozen until ready to use, which makes them the perfect party food.

For the kofta

¼ cup (20 g) panko bread crumbs

¼ cup (60 ml) milk

2 tablespoons extra-virgin olive oil

½ yellow onion, diced

4 cloves garlic, sliced

1 teaspoon ground coriander

1 teaspoon ground cumin

½ teaspoon ground allspice

½ teaspoon ground cinnamon

¼ teaspoon cayenne pepper

¼ teaspoon ground ginger

¼ teaspoon freshly ground black pepper

1½ teaspoons kosher salt

1 pound (455 g) ground beef

½ bunch fresh parsley, minced

For the shawarma sauce

1 cup (240 ml) Greek yogurt

¼ cup (60 ml) mayonnaise

¼ cup (60 ml) tahini

Juice of 1 lemon

3 cloves garlic, grated

2 tablespoons minced fresh dill

1 teaspoon kosher salt

½ teaspoon freshly ground black pepper

ingredients continue

MAKE THE KOFTA

In a small bowl, combine the panko and the milk and set aside for about 10 minutes.

In a small sauté pan, heat the oil over medium-high heat. Once the oil is hot, add the onion and garlic and cook until the onion is translucent, about 4 minutes. Set aside to cool.

In a small bowl, mix together the ground coriander, cumin, allspice, cinnamon, cayenne, ginger, black pepper, and salt. Place the ground beef and parsley in a large bowl. Add the spice blend, cooled onion and garlic, and the soaked panko. Mix everything together until well combined.

Divide the kofta mixture into 6 equal portions. Place one of the portions onto a piece of plastic wrap. Roll the plastic wrap around the piece of meat to make a sausage shape. Wrap it tight and place into the refrigerator or freezer to set the shape. Repeat this step for all the portions of kofta.

MAKE THE SHAWARMA SAUCE

In a small bowl, stir together the yogurt, mayonnaise, tahini, lemon juice, garlic, dill, salt, and pepper. Set aside until serving time.

SET UP THE GRILL

Preheat a charcoal or gas grill to medium-high heat with a target temperature of 400°F (205°C).

Remove the kofta from the refrigerator and take off the plastic wrap. Thread each one onto a skewer. Thread the sliced eggplant onto the other skewers, one after the other, using two skewers for each one to stabilize if necessary. Brush the eggplant with 2 tablespoons of the olive oil and season with salt and pepper.

recipe continues

For grilling

10 wooden skewers (soaked for at least 20 minutes)

2 Japanese eggplants, thinly sliced into rounds

2 tablespoons extra-virgin olive oil, plus more for green onions

Kosher salt and freshly ground black pepper

1 bunch green onions

6 pita breads, store-bought or homemade (page 66)

For serving

¼ cup (60 ml) extra-virgin olive oil

3 to 4 large Roma tomatoes, sliced

½ bunch fresh oregano, leaves picked

Juice of 1 lemon

Kosher salt and freshly ground black pepper

Fresh mint, for garnish

Once the grill is hot, place the kofta kebabs onto the grill. You can either place them directly onto the grill or onto a cast-iron flattop griddle. Rotate the kebabs every minute or so to cook evenly on all sides. Add the eggplant skewers to the grill at the same time and cook everything for 10 to 12 minutes, turning frequently for even cooking. While you're grilling, rub the green onions with a little bit of oil and throw them on the grill, cooking until nicely charred.

Once the kofta are cooked and nicely browned, remove from the grill and set aside to rest for a couple minutes.

Place the pita breads on the grill just long enough to heat them through and make them pliable.

TO SERVE

Remove the eggplant from the skewers and place in a serving bowl. Add the olive oil, tomatoes, oregano, and lemon juice. Toss well and season to taste with salt and pepper.

Arrange the kofta kebabs, grilled pita, grilled green onions, and mint on a platter. Pour the shawarma sauce into a small serving bowl with a spoon. Serve warm, instructing diners to assemble their own sandwiches.

STEAKS
AND
CHOPS

IF THE QUICK FIRE CHAPTER IS WHERE I THINK YOU MIGHT SPEND THE MOST TIME, THIS STEAKS AND CHOPS CHAPTER IS WHERE I SPEND MUCH OF MINE. And it makes perfect sense, given the fact that after all these years, what I have found the most passion for is cooking great steaks. It's why I decided to open Miller & Lux, and having spent years crafting a dry-aged beef program and executing nightly plates of my favorite cuts, I can say with authority that I think I've perfected the technique . . . and you can, too. Here's the thing—and this isn't news to anyone: When you start with an amazing product, you need to do very little to it to get an amazing outcome. Most of the steaks and chops in the pages to come are seasoned with little more than salt and pepper and finished with coarse salt and extra-virgin olive oil (or Steak Oil, page 241). Most of them cook quickly, and most go with pretty much any side dish. So this will always be a great place to start.

RARE

MEDIUM-RARE

MEDIUM

MEDIUM-WELL

WELL DONE

GRILLED NEW YORK STRIP STEAK

SERVES 2

New York strip is a steak lover's steak. What I mean by that is that it has a denser, toothier quality to it—you need to want to chew. It straddles the line between a rib eye and a filet: not as fatty as the first and not as lean as the latter. It's a great slicing steak to share, so I'll often think about recommending this one when I'm serving a table for two. When cooked properly, this needs only a sprinkle of salt and some chopped fresh chives to make it shine.

1 New York strip steak (20 ounces/570 g)

Extra-virgin olive oil

Kosher salt and freshly ground black pepper

2 tablespoons Steak Oil (page 241)

Maldon sea salt, for garnish

Minced fresh chives, for garnish

Pull the steak out of the refrigerator 1 to 2 hours before cooking to take the chill off.

SET UP THE GRILL

Preheat a charcoal or gas grill to medium-high heat, and set it up with two zones: a hot side and cold (less hot) side, for direct and indirect cooking. (See method, page 15.) You want the temperature to hover around 400°F (205°C).

Place the steak onto a tray lined with paper towels and pat dry. Rub with a little bit of olive oil, just enough to allow the salt to stick to it. Season with plenty of salt and place the steak on the hot side of the grill. Cook until the steak has a nice even sear on it with even browning, 4 to 5 minutes. Flip the steak over and cook on the other side for another 4 to 5 minutes. Move the steak to the cooler side of the grill, close the lid, and cook until the desired temperature is reached, about 125°F (52°C) for medium-rare (see temperature chart, page 126).

Season with the pepper and slice the steak off the bone. Going against the grain and with the knife at an angle to the cutting board, cut the steak into ¼-inch (6 mm) slices so the pieces can shingle away from each other. Place the slices in a nice line on a plate or platter and drizzle with some steak oil. Garnish with a sprinkle of Maldon salt and fresh chives. Serve hot.

GRILLED FILET MIGNON

SERVES 1 OR 2

The grilled filet mignon steak is the true definition of culinary opulence: the most tender, most elegantly succulent cut that feels like it's meant for an occasion. This one pairs beautifully with the Bordelaise Sauce (page 244), and I love it simply served with a good salad and M&L Potato Puree (page 207).

1 center-cut filet mignon (10 ounce/280 g)

Extra-virgin olive oil

Kosher salt and freshly ground black pepper

Pull the steak out of the refrigerator 1 to 2 hours before cooking to take the chill off.

SET UP THE GRILL

Preheat a charcoal or gas grill to medium-high heat, and set it up with two zones: a hot side and cold (less hot) side, for direct and indirect cooking. (See method, page 15.) You want the temperature to hover around 400°F (205°C).

Place the steak onto a tray lined with paper towels and pat dry. Rub with a little bit of olive oil, just enough to allow the salt to stick to it. Season with the salt and place the steak on the hot side of the grill. Cook until the steak has a nice even sear on it with even browning, 4 to 5 minutes. Flip the steak over and cook on the other side for another 4 to 5 minutes. Move the steak to the cooler side of the grill, close the lid, and cook until the desired temperature is reached, about 125°F (52°C) for medium-rare (see temperature chart, page 126).

Remove the steak from the grill and season with pepper. Let rest on a rack or plate for 8 to 10 minutes before serving. Place the filet on a plate and serve with your favorite steak sauce and sides.

GRILLED PORK CHOPS WITH HERB BUTTER

SERVES 4 TO 6

Brine these thicker pork chops to keep them from drying out—even though it feels like an extra step, I promise it's worth the effort. A lemon-herb compound butter adds an extra layer of moisture and flavor. Make the butter ahead of time and keep it in the fridge to top not only these chops but any steak or seafood in the book. We like serving these with the Campfire Potatoes (page 184).

For the brined pork chops

¾ cups (165 g) brown sugar

¾ cups (100 g) kosher salt

1 teaspoon black peppercorns

1 teaspoon coriander seeds

3 to 4 sprigs fresh thyme

4 cloves garlic, smashed and peeled

1 lemon, sliced

4 to 6 bone-in pork chops (12 to 16 ounces/340 to 455 g each), about 1½ inches (4 cm) thick

Kosher salt and freshly ground black pepper

For the herb butter

4 tablespoons (57 g) unsalted butter

1 bunch fresh chives, minced

¼ bunch fresh parsley, minced

Juice of ½ lemon

Kosher salt and freshly ground black pepper

BRINE THE PORK CHOPS

In a large bowl, combine 4 cups (960 ml) lukewarm water, the brown sugar, and salt and whisk until completely dissolved. Add the peppercorns, coriander seeds, thyme, garlic, and lemon slices. Add the pork chops to the bowl, making sure that they are completely covered by the liquid. Set aside for 1 hour.

SET UP THE GRILL

Preheat a charcoal or gas grill to medium-high heat, and set it up with two zones: a hot side and cold (less hot) side, for direct and indirect cooking. (See method, page 15.) You want the temperature to hover around 400°F (205°C).

Remove the pork chops from the brine. Place them on a tray or plate lined with paper towels and dry completely. Season with salt and pepper and place onto the hot side of the grill. Grill for 2 to 3 minutes per side, getting some good-looking grill marks on them. Transfer the chops to the cooler side of the grill and continue to cook, rotating every minute or so, until they come to an internal temperature of 135°F (57°C), 3 to 4 minutes per side more.

MEANWHILE, MAKE THE HERB BUTTER

Place a small grill-safe pot over the hot side of the grill. Add the butter into the pot just until melted. Remove the pot from the grill and fold in the chives, parsley, and lemon juice. Season with salt and pepper and set aside.

Once the chops are fully cooked, remove from the grill and top them with the herb butter. Let rest for about 5 minutes before serving.

PESTO-GRILLED SKIRT STEAK

SERVES 4 TO 6

There are dishes that reinvent the wheel (see Smoked Beef Ribs Bourguignon, page 158) and then there are dishes like this one, necessities for any cook's repertoire. This is one of those recipes that you can make for dinner either on a Tuesday or for weekend company, that you'll know how to do by memory—the technique, at least—after you've made it once or twice. I love to serve this dish with the Grilled Ratatouille (page 188) you see in the photo.

1 skirt steak (2 pounds/910 g), trimmed and
   cleaned
¼ to ½ cup (60 to 120 ml) Fresh Herb Pesto
   (page 240)
Fresh parsley, for garnish
Fresh basil leaves, for garnish
Flaky sea salt, for garnish
Parmesan cheese, for garnish

SET UP THE GRILL

Preheat a charcoal or gas grill to medium-high heat, and set it up with two zones: a hot side and cold (less hot) side, for direct and indirect cooking. (See method, page 15.) You want the temperature to hover around 400°F (205°C).

Remove the steak from the package and dry very well on paper towels to remove any excess moisture. Rub the steak liberally with the pesto.

Place the steak over the hot side of the grill until a nice char is formed on the steak, 3 to 5 minutes. Flip the steak and repeat on the other side for another 3 to 5 minutes. Move the steak to the cooler side of the grill, close the lid, and cook until the steak reaches an internal temperature of 132°F (56°C), another 4 to 5 minutes. Remove the steak from the grill and let rest for 8 to 10 minutes before slicing against the grain.

Place the steak on a large platter and garnish with fresh parsley and basil leaves, flaky sea salt, and freshly grated Parmesan cheese.

BULGOGI BEEF BOWLS

SERVES 4 TO 6

I love cooking the beef for these vibrant Korean-inspired bowls over a yakitori grill, which looks like a portable charcoal-filled box with a grid-like rack over the top. It feels like such an approachable way to cook over charcoal, and the beef gets a great crispy char as it cooks. Of course, if you don't have one, this will do well over any type of grill, and the real star of the recipe is the spicy, savory beef marinade. The flavors are balanced out by a bright cucumber salad and other fresh garnishes (and oozing fried eggs) that all go over a fragrant ginger rice.

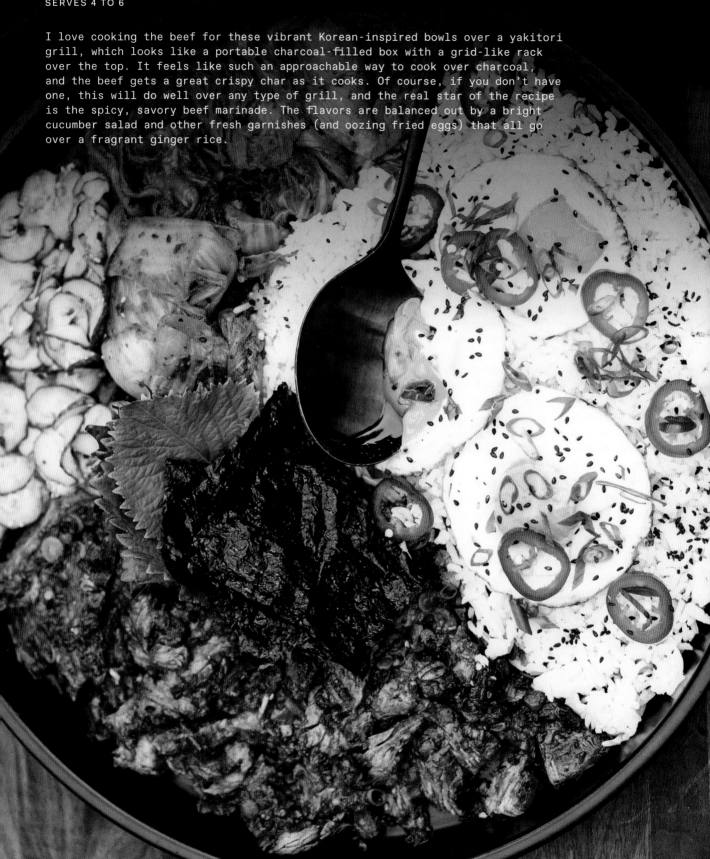

For the marinated steak

½ cup (120 ml) soy sauce

2 tablespoons rice vinegar

Grated zest and juice of 1 lemon

2 tablespoons gochujang (Korean chile paste)

2 tablespoons light brown sugar

2 tablespoons sesame oil

1 teaspoon minced fresh ginger

3 green onions, white and light-green parts only, thinly sliced

3 cloves garlic, minced

1 Fresno chile, sliced

½ tablespoon chile flakes

Freshly ground black pepper

2-pound (910 g) skirt steak

For the cucumber salad

¼ cup (60 ml) rice vinegar

2 tablespoons mirin

1 teaspoon sesame seeds

1 teaspoon sambal oelek

½ teaspoon kosher salt

½ English cucumber, thinly shaved

For the ginger rice

2 cups (455 g) long-grain white rice

1 knob fresh ginger, peeled and halved lengthwise

2 cloves garlic, smashed and peeled

4 tablespoons (60 g) unsalted butter

2 teaspoons kosher salt

For the bowls

4 to 6 fried eggs (1 per serving)

Kimchi

Sliced green onions, for garnish

Sliced Fresno chiles, for garnish

Nori (seaweed) squares, for garnish

Gochujang (Korean chile paste), for serving

MARINATE THE STEAK

In a large bowl or zip-seal storage bag, mix together the soy sauce, vinegar, lemon zest, lemon juice, gochujang, brown sugar, sesame oil, ginger, green onions, garlic, Fresno chile, and chile flakes. Season with some black pepper and stir until well combined. Add the skirt steak and toss to coat evenly. Marinate for at least 2 hours, or up to overnight.

MAKE THE CUCUMBER SALAD

In a medium bowl, stir together the vinegar, mirin, sesame seeds, sambal, and salt. Toss the cucumbers in and set aside until ready to use. You can do this ahead of time and refrigerate up to overnight.

MAKE THE RICE

In a medium saucepan, combine 4 cups (960 ml) water, the rice, ginger, garlic, butter, and salt. Set the pot over medium-high heat and once the rice begins to boil, cover the pot and reduce the heat to low. Simmer on low for 15 minutes. Once cooked, use a fork to fluff the rice.

SET UP THE GRILL

While the rice is cooking, preheat a charcoal or gas grill to medium-high heat, and set it up with two zones: a hot side and cold (less hot) side, for direct and indirect cooking. (See method, page 15.) You want the temperature to hover around 400°F (205°C).

Place the steak over the hot side of the grill until a nice char is formed on the steak, 3 to 5 minutes. Flip the steak and repeat on the other side for another 3 to 5 minutes. Move the steak to the cooler side of the grill, close the lid, and cook until the steak reaches an internal temperature of 132°F (56°C), another 4 to 5 minutes. Remove the steak from the grill and let rest for 8 to 10 minutes before slicing against the grain.

ASSEMBLE THE BOWLS

Divide the rice among four to six bowls and top with a portion of sliced steak, cucumber salad, a fried egg, and your desired number of garnishes. Serve immediately, with extra gochujang on the side.

SANTA MARIA–STYLE TRI-TIP

SERVES 4 TO 6

If there are four pillars of barbecue in the American tradition—Memphis, Kansas City, the Carolinas, and Texas—central California barbecue is the fifth, and Santa Maria-style tri-tip is arguably the representative dish. Typically served with small pinquito beans, the slower-cooked cut has become an art form. We serve this version with juicy cherry tomatoes and red onions to help brighten it.

For the steak

2 teaspoons dried oregano

2 teaspoons garlic powder

2 teaspoons onion powder

2 teaspoons smoked paprika

2 teaspoons ground coriander

2 teaspoons ground cumin

3 teaspoons kosher salt

1 teaspoon freshly ground black pepper

¼ cup (60 ml) extra-virgin olive oil

1 tri-tip steak (2½ to 3 pounds/1.2 to 1.4 kg)

For the vegetables

2 tablespoons extra-virgin olive oil

1 large red onion, sliced

1 pound (455 g) cherry tomatoes (still on the vine or loose)

Kosher salt and freshly ground black pepper

4 to 6 sprigs fresh oregano

For the chimichurri sauce

2 tablespoons minced shallot

2 tablespoons fresh lime juice

2 tablespoons distilled white vinegar

½ teaspoon chile flakes

½ teaspoon sugar

1 jalapeño, minced

¾ bunch fresh oregano leaves, minced, plus extra for garnish

½ bunch fresh parsley leaves, minced

½ cup (120 ml) extra-virgin olive oil

Kosher salt and freshly ground black pepper

For serving

Oregano leaves, for garnish

Lime wedges, for squeezing

Cooked pinto or other beans (optional)

RUB THE STEAK

In a bowl, combine all the herbs, spices, salt, pepper, and olive oil and mix well. Coat the steak using all the rub and set aside, covered, for at least 1 hour.

SET UP THE GRILL

Preheat a charcoal or gas grill to medium-high heat, and set it up with two zones: a hot side and cold (less hot) side, for direct and indirect cooking. (See method, page 15.) You want the temperature to hover around 400°F (205°C).

GRILL THE STEAK AND VEGETABLES

Place the steak on the hot side of the grill for 2 to 3 minutes per side. Let it get some nice color and char and then move to the cooler side of the grill. Cook on the cooler side, flipping halfway through, until it reaches an internal temperature of 125°F (52°C) for medium-rare for 35 to 40 minutes. If you like it more medium-well, cook to 135°F (57°C). Let rest for about 10 minutes before slicing.

When the steak has 15 to 20 minutes left, place a cast-iron skillet on the hot side of the grill. When hot, add the olive oil, along with the onions and tomatoes. Season with salt and pepper and place a few sprigs of oregano over the top. Let the vegetables cook while the steak continues to cook, stirring occasionally.

MAKE THE CHIMICHURRI SAUCE

In a small bowl, combine the shallot, lime juice, vinegar, chile flakes, sugar, and jalapeño and mix. Let sit for 5 to 10 minutes before folding in the oregano, parsley, and olive oil. Season with salt and pepper. Set aside.

TO SERVE

Slice the steak against the grain into thin slices. Place on a platter with the onions and tomatoes and spoon the chimichurri sauce over the top. Garnish with a few extra oregano leaves and some cut limes. Serve with pinto or other cooked beans, if desired.

GRILLED TOMAHAWK RIB EYE

SERVES 3 OR 4

This is far and away the most popular wow-factor signature dish we serve at Miller & Lux. Presented with its giant Flintstones-style bone, the beauty of this cut, which we dry-age for forty-five days, is the sheer size—three or four people can happily enjoy it for dinner along with a few side dishes. This isn't necessarily a cut that will be sitting in the butcher counter, so you may have to order it ahead of time.

1 Tomahawk rib-eye steak, dry-aged if
    possible
Kosher salt and freshly ground black pepper
Steak Oil (optional; page 241) or extra-virgin
    olive oil, for drizzling
Coarse sea salt, such as Maldon, for garnish
Snipped fresh chives, for garnish

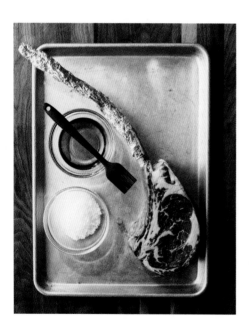

SET UP THE GRILL

Preheat a charcoal or gas grill to medium-high heat, and set it up with two zones: a hot side and cold (less hot) side, for direct and indirect cooking. (See method, page 15.) You want the temperature to hover around 400°F (205°C).

As the grill heats, allow the steak to come to room temperature. Pat the steak dry and season with salt and pepper. Wrap the bone in aluminum foil.

Place the steak on the hot side of the grill until you have nice grill marks, 3 to 4 minutes. Flip the steak and repeat. Once it has good color, place on the cooler side of the grill, close the lid, and continue to cook, flipping halfway through, until the internal temperature reaches 125°F (52°C) for medium-rare, 3 to 6 minutes. This is my recommendation for this particular cut, but leave the meat on for longer to achieve your desired doneness (see temperature chart, page 126).

Let the steak rest 8 to 10 minutes before slicing. Slice the steak off the bone and then cut against the grain across the rib eye. Serve drizzled with steak oil (or extra-virgin olive oil, for ease) and garnish with coarse sea salt and snipped chives.

WHOLE BEEF TENDERLOIN

SERVES 6 TO 8

Something I learned back in my New York days in the late 1990s is that the art of true sophistication can be really simple—it doesn't necessarily need to be dynamic. Case in point is this elegant beef tenderloin, which gets seasoned with just salt and pepper and brushed with a combination of Dijon mustard and thyme. The sweet floral nature of the fresh herb matches with the punchy notes of Dijon, and that's honestly all you need. The method here is more of a reverse-sear, where you start on the cooler side of the grill first and move the tenderloin over to the hot side at the end to get your crust. Use an herb brush (page 21) to baste extra mustard mix onto the meat as it cooks.

1 cup (240 ml) Dijon mustard

1 cup (240 ml) coarse-grain mustard

½ cup (120 ml) extra-virgin olive oil

2 tablespoons chopped fresh thyme, plus more for garnish

Kosher salt and freshly ground black pepper

1 beef tenderloin (3 pounds/1.4 kg)

Coarse sea salt, such as Maldon, for garnish

SET UP THE GRILL

Preheat a charcoal or gas grill to medium-high heat, and set it up with two zones: a hot side and cold (less hot) side, for direct and indirect cooking. (See method, page 15.) You want the temperature to hover around 400°F (205°C).

In a small bowl, stir together both mustards, the oil, and thyme. Add a generous amount of salt and pepper and thin with a few tablespoons of water, if necessary, to make the mixture loosely spreadable. Spread half of the mixture over all sides of the tenderloin.

Place the steak on the cooler side of the grill and let it slowly come to temperature, turning occasionally. Continue to cook, basting occasionally with more of the mustard sauce, until the tenderloin reaches an internal temperature of 112° to 115°F (44° to 46°C), about 45 minutes. In the last 5 to 10 minutes of cooking, move the tenderloin over to the hot side of the grill, to get some char on the exterior. Remove when the internal temp of the steak reaches 125°F (52°C) for medium-rare; leave on longer if you want it cooked further.

Rest for 10 to 15 minutes, then slice into steaks. Garnish with fresh thyme and sprinkle with coarse sea salt. Serve immediately with any remaining mustard sauce.

GRILLED RACK OF LAMB WITH MINT SALSA VERDE AND PISTACHIO CRUMBLE

SERVES 6 TO 8

Take this recipe as a sign to grab that rack of lamb in the grocery case you always see but don't know how to use. If the butcher will french the chops (clean the ends of the bones) for you, all the better. This is a great additional protein option for when the mood strikes. It feels elevated for a weeknight meal, but cooks quickly enough—in under 30 minutes—to be just that.

For the mint salsa verde

2 cups (60 g) fresh mint leaves

1½ cups (45 g) fresh parsley leaves

½ cup (15 g) fresh tarragon leaves

1 tablespoon capers, drained

1 clove garlic, peeled

3 oil-packed anchovy fillets

Grated zest of 1 lemon

Juice of ½ lemon

½ cup (120 ml) extra-virgin olive oil

Kosher salt and freshly ground black pepper

1 Fresno chile, finely diced, plus more
    for garnish

For the lamb

2 racks of lamb (16 chops total), frenched

Extra-virgin olive oil

Kosher salt and freshly ground black pepper

¾ cup (95 g) pistachios, toasted and coarsely
    chopped

MAKE THE MINT SALSA VERDE

In a food processor or high-powered blender, pulse the herbs, capers, garlic, anchovy, lemon zest, lemon juice, and olive oil until you have a coarse puree. Season to taste with salt and pepper and fold in the chiles. Set aside.

SET UP THE GRILL

Preheat a charcoal or gas grill to medium-high heat, and set it up with two zones: a hot side and cold (less hot) side, for direct and indirect cooking. (See method, page 15.) You want the temperature to hover around 400°F (205°C).

Cover the exposed part of the lamb bones in foil. Rub the meat with olive oil and season well with salt and pepper. Place the lamb on the hot side of the grill and cook for 6 to 7 minutes. Flip the racks and cook for 5 minutes more. Move to the cooler side of the grill, close the lid, and cook until the internal temperature reaches 125°F (52°C) for medium-rare, another 15 minutes or so.

Cut the lamb into double chops, with 2 bones in each chop. Place on a platter and spoon the salsa verde over the top. Garnish with sliced Fresno chiles and the chopped pistachios and serve immediately.

LOW
AND
SLOW

ONCE YOU'VE BECOME AN ENTHUSIAST ON THE GRILL—AND FOR OUTDOOR COOKING IN GENERAL—THE NEXT LOGICAL STEP IS TO DIVE INTO THE WORLD OF SMOKING. That means either setting up a smoking component right in your grill or going one step further and buying a stand-alone smoker. Some will require you to babysit the coals and burning wood all day, though others—like electric or pellet smokers—have made it much easier to set and forget. I'll tell you, there are few things more satisfying than cutting into a juicy brisket that you've been cooking for twelve hours or pulling apart ribs with your fingers that have smoked long enough so the meat literally falls right off the bone. These are the projects of this book—the labors of love that you'll try on a Sunday morning to have in time for dinner, or that you'll plan an entire party around. They'll fill your yard with the evocative smell of burning hickory or applewood. And they'll usually yield enough to give you leftovers, making the act of true patience totally worth the payoff.

SMOKED BRISKET

SERVES 10 TO 12

Texas-style smoked brisket is the holy grail of American BBQ, and it's not so much about cooking as it is babysitting. If you're willing to put in the time, the result is so, so worth it. Start early and as the internal temperature of the brisket starts to increase, don't get impatient with the "stall" that happens around 140°F (60°C). The most important thing is maintaining an even box temp between 225° and 250°F (110° and 120°C). This is where you should rely on those tips in Maintaining the Temperature (page 17). Let the brisket rest for at least an hour, wrapped, before you cut into it: This allows the tense muscles to relax, and it's how you'll get that pinnacle melt-in-your-mouth texture.

For the smoked brisket

1 brisket (12 pounds/5.4 kg)
1½ cups Brisket Chile Spice Rub (page 245)
Smoker Spritz (page 239)

For serving

BBQ Sauce (page 238)
Sliced white sandwich bread
Bread and butter pickles
Pickled Red Onions (page 95)
Marge's Potato Salad (page 192)

PREPARE THE BRISKET

Trim the brisket, but leave ¼ to ½ inch (6 to 12 mm) of fat on top. Rub the spice rub over both sides of the brisket. Wrap tightly in plastic wrap. Place in the refrigerator and let sit overnight.

Very early in the morning, remove the brisket from the refrigerator and let sit while you set up the smoker.

SET UP THE SMOKER

Preheat the smoker to 250°F (120°C).

Place the brisket into a large pan. Rub a little warm water onto the brisket and season liberally with the spice rub.

Place the brisket into the smoker. Check the meat after about 5 hours. Tilt the brisket to remove any fat from pooling on it. Spritz liberally and close the smoker.

After another 4 hours, check the temperature of the brisket. Once it hits about 185°F (85°C) it is ready to wrap.

WRAP THE BRISKET

Place butcher paper down on the table and spray with the spritz. This will help make the paper easier to wrap. Place the brisket on the paper and wrap tightly.

Place the brisket back into the smoker and cook until an internal temperature of 205°F (95°C) is achieved.

Wrap the brisket, still wrapped in the paper, in an old towel. Place the wrapped brisket into a sealed cooler to improve the texture and let rest for at least 2 hours.

When ready to eat, slice the brisket against the grain. Serve on a platter with BBQ sauce, sandwich bread, pickles, pickled onions, and potato salad.

SMOKED PORK SHOULDER WITH MAPLE SWEET POTATOES

SERVES 8 TO 10

Pork and sweet potatoes have been friends for a very long time, and there's a good reason for that. Savory pork always wants something with a little sugar content to balance it out—you'll often see apples alongside the protein— and vibrant yams are another great option. Here, we add a smoky element to connect the dots between the two, and it feels like a slam dunk. The potatoes cook while the pork is finishing and get a twice-smoked treatment that's unexpected and fun.

For the pork shoulder

2 tablespoons coriander seeds

2 tablespoons fennel seeds

1 tablespoon freshly ground black pepper

Grated zest of 2 oranges

1 teaspoon chile flakes

1½ tablespoons kosher salt

¼ cup (60 ml) extra-virgin olive oil

1 boneless pork shoulder (4½ pounds/2 kg)

Smoker Spritz (page 239)

For the sweet potatoes

8 small to medium sweet potatoes, poked
   with a fork

2 sticks (8 ounces/225 g) unsalted butter,
   at room temperature

3 tablespoons maple syrup

1 teaspoon ground coriander

Grated zest of 1 orange

½ cup (50 g) grated Parmesan cheese,
   plus more for garnish

2 tablespoons minced fresh chives, plus
   more for garnish

1½ tablespoons kosher salt

SET UP THE SMOKER
Preheat a smoker to 250°F (120°C); see instructions on page 16.

PREPARE THE PORK
With a mortar and pestle or spice grinder, crush the coriander seeds, fennel seeds, and pepper together until finely ground. Transfer to a bowl and mix in the orange zest, chile flakes, salt, and olive oil. Rub all over the pork. Place the smoker spritz in a spray bottle.

SMOKE THE PORK
Place the pork into the smoker and cook until the internal temperature reaches 165°F (74°C). Throughout the smoke time, spritz the pork occasionally with the smoker spritz to retain moisture. Pull the pork shoulder from the smoker, wrap well in butcher paper, and place back inside until the internal temperature reaches 190°F (88°C). This whole process will take 6 to 7 hours total. Remove the pork and let it rest before slicing.

COOK THE SWEET POTATOES
About 3 hours before the pork is done, start the potatoes. Place the poked potatoes into the smoker with the pork. Cook until tender, about 2 hours.

While the potatoes are cooking, in a medium bowl, stir together the butter, maple syrup, ground coriander, orange zest, Parmesan, chives, and salt.

Halve the potatoes and scrape the flesh out into a bowl (hold on to the skins). Mix with the compound butter while still hot. Spoon the flesh back into the potato skins and place back in the smoker for another 30 minutes. When finished, garnish with more Parmesan and minced chives.

Serve the sliced pork and sweet potatoes together.

ULTIMATE BARBECUE RIBS

SERVES 6 TO 8

If you're going use this book for one recipe, this is it. Knowing how to master the art of perfectly smoked ribs is the gateway drug to barbecue and smoking, and I promise you, once you've turned out a few racks of these meltingly tender, fall-off-the-bone bad boys, you'll be converted. The recipe for the rub makes more than you need before smoking, but you'll also want to shake some on the finished ribs. (Store the rest in an airtight container and use for more ribs . . . or chicken or beef.)

2 racks St. Louis–style spare ribs
Rib and Chicken Dry Rub (page 244)
Smoker Spritz (page 239)
BBQ Sauce (page 238)

Score the membrane on the back side (bone side) of the ribs with a paring knife. This will allow the smoke to penetrate the meat through the membrane.

Pat the ribs dry and rub generously with the rib rub on all sides. Let sit about 15 minutes to allow the rub to set in.

SET UP THE SMOKER
Preheat a smoker to 250 to 275°F (120 to 135°C).

FIRST COOK ON THE RIBS
Place the ribs into the smoker with the meat side facing up and the bones facing down. Set a timer for 1½ hours, spritzing every 30 minutes.

SECOND COOK ON THE RIBS
Place a large piece of foil onto a table. Place the ribs onto the foil, meat side down. Tightly wrap the foil up around the ribs and place them back into the smoker for another 1½ hours, or until the internal temperature of the meat hits 205°F (95°C). Pull the ribs out, unwrap them, and let them rest for about 30 minutes.

THIRD COOK ON THE RIBS
Brush the ribs with the BBQ sauce and place back onto the grill or smoker for 10 to 15 minutes to set the sauce. Finish with more rib rub, slice, and serve.

SMOKED CHICKEN, TWO WAYS

EACH CHICKEN SERVES 4

I always think of smoked chicken as the perfect thing to round out a summertime menu, an addition to other meats as opposed to the main event. Because it can be a bit of a project to fire up the smoker, many find it easier to do the quick-cooking chicken elsewhere. But I like to think of it as a "plus one." Spending all day doing a brisket or tending to ribs? Throw a couple chickens in the smoker, too—leftovers are perfect the next day, and nobody is mad about a smoky drumstick on the table. Here are two of our favorite ways to get this done.

2 whole chickens (3½ to 5 pounds/1.6 to 2.3 kg each), spatchcocked (see Note)

Version 1

½ cup (75 g) Rib and Chicken Dry Rub (page 244)

Version 2

Reverse-Sear Dry Brine (page 238)

PREP THE CHICKEN

Rub the dry rub or dry brine all over the chickens, making sure to coat completely. Let sit while the smoker heats up.

SET UP THE SMOKER

Preheat a smoker to 225° to 250°F (110° to 120°C); see the instructions on page 16.

Place the chickens directly on the smoker racks and smoke until the internal temperature reaches 160°F (71°C), about 3 hours.

Set aside to rest for 20 minutes. Cut into pieces and serve immediately.

Note: You can either ask the butcher to spatchcock the chicken for you or do it at home. Here's how: Using sharp kitchen shears or a very sharp knife, cut along either side of the backbone from the neck to the tail end and pull it out. Make a small slit in the cartilage at the bottom end of the breast bones (it covers the dark keel bone underneath). With both hands placed on the rib cage, crack open the chicken by opening it, like a book, toward the cutting board. This will reveal the keel bone. Run your fingers up along either side of the cartilage in between the breasts to loosen it from the flesh. Grab the keel bone and pull up to remove it, along with the attached cartilage. Flip over and smooth the skin before continuing with the recipe.

SMOKED SALMON BAGEL BOARD

SERVES 8

This is where you should head for Sunday brunch—a quick kipper-style smoked salmon that makes for a spectacular, showstopping presentation as part of a bagel board or brunch spread. Serve with cream cheese and all the toppings—tomatoes, onions, capers, dill, the works—for a great DIY midmorning party. The salmon cooks quickly and will hold for several days in the fridge.

For the smoked salmon

¼ cup (35 g) kosher salt

1 tablespoon plus 1 teaspoon brown sugar

2 tablespoons chopped fresh dill

Grated zest of 2 lemons

1 side of salmon (3 to 4 pounds/1.4 to 1.8 kg)

For the bagel board

8 bagels

1 pound (455 g) cream cheese (flavors of choice)

Sliced tomatoes

Sliced cucumbers

Sliced onions

Capers

Fresh dill

Lemon wedges

SET UP THE SMOKER

Preheat a smoker to 250°F (120°C); see the instructions on page 16.

SMOKE THE SALMON

In a small bowl, mix together the salt, brown sugar, dill, and lemon zest. Rub all over the flesh of the salmon, coating evenly. Place directly onto the rack in the smoker and cook until the fish is cooked through and flakes easily with a fork, 45 minutes to 1 hour.

ASSEMBLE THE BAGEL BOARD

Arrange the salmon on a platter with the bagels, cream cheese, sliced tomatoes, sliced cucumbers, sliced onions, capers, dill, and lemon wedges (or any combination of the above).

SMOKED BEEF RIBS BOURGUIGNON

SERVES 4

This recipe started in one place and ended up somewhere completely different, which is often the most fun part of development. I knew I wanted smoked beef ribs, and I knew I wanted them in a porcini rub. But beyond that, we had to figure out how to add more mushrooms to the recipe, keep the smoky characteristics of the ribs, and ensure that they were tender. What resulted was a dish that finally found its soul, this innovative hybrid smoke-braise, which incorporates our favorite things about meaty barbecue and warming mushroom Bourguignon. The rich gravy gives the tender ribs their purpose. This is most definitely a weekend project as opposed to a quick weeknight dish. But it's unlike anything you've experienced, I guarantee it.

For the ribs

1 cup Porcini Mushroom Rub (page 245)

3½ pounds (1.6 kg) bone-in beef short ribs

Smoker Spritz (page 239)

For the braising liquid

4 slices bacon

4 sprigs fresh thyme

10 ounces (280 g) frozen pearl onions, thawed

8 ounces (225 g) cremini mushrooms, halved

2 large carrots, peeled and cut into ¼-inch (6 mm) coins

Kosher salt and freshly ground black pepper

2 cups (480 ml) dry red wine

2 cups (480 ml) reduced-sodium beef broth

3 tablespoons (45 g) unsalted butter

RUB THE RIBS

Coat the outsides of the short ribs with the rub.

SET UP THE SMOKER

Preheat a smoker to 225° to 250°F (110° to 120°C); see instructions on page 16. Add the ribs to the smoker. While the ribs start to cook, place the spritz in a spray bottle. Smoke until the ribs get soft but still hold their shape, about 4 hours, spritzing the meat with the vinegar solution every 30 minutes. Set aside.

MEANWHILE, MAKE THE BRAISING LIQUID

Line a plate with paper towels. Layer the bacon into a Dutch oven, set over medium heat, and cook the bacon until the fat is released and the meat is crisp and browned, turning a few times during cooking, about 10 minutes. Remove the bacon to the paper towels and set aside. Once cool, slice the bacon into ¼-inch (6 mm) lardons.

Add a few of the thyme sprigs to the Dutch oven and increase the heat to medium-high. Add the pearl onions, mushrooms, and carrots. Season with salt and pepper and cook until the vegetables are lightly browned, stirring often during cooking, 6 to 8 minutes. Remove the vegetables and herbs to a plate with a slotted spoon. Cover and set aside.

Add the red wine to the pot and bring to a boil, scraping up any browned bits from the bottom of the pot. Let boil and reduce for 1 minute. Add the beef broth and bring back to a boil. Remove from the heat and tuck the smoked ribs into the sauce. Cover the pot with a heavy tight-fitting lid or a few layers of heavy-duty foil. Return to the smoker and cook until the meat is very tender, 2½ to 3 hours more. Keep the smoker temperature at 225°F (110°C) by adding charcoal as necessary, but do not add more chips.

Use tongs to gently remove the ribs from the pot, placing them on a warm platter. Wrap tightly with foil and a couple of kitchen towels to keep them warm while you make the sauce.

Strain the braising liquid from the Dutch oven into another pot, discarding the remaining solids. Set it over medium-high heat and cook, undisturbed, until reduced and thickened, about 10 minutes. Remove from the heat. Add the butter and whisk it in to make the sauce thick and glossy. Taste and season with salt and pepper accordingly.

Unwrap the ribs and add them to the sauce along with the cooked vegetables. Gently toss everything to combine and warm through and then serve, garnished with the remaining fresh thyme.

CITRUS-SMOKED SPATCHCOCKED TURKEY

SERVES 8 TO 10

Let's be honest. You're only making this one day of the year—you can pretend otherwise, but you know it's true. That being said, if you're trying to make a turkey that stands out, look no further. Easier than deep-frying, more exciting than a traditional roast, this one bridges the gap between approachable and just different enough to make it fun. Serve it with your favorite gravy and sides, and don't forget to make enough for leftovers.

1 whole turkey (12 to 14 pounds/5.4 to 6.4 kg)

4 whole tangerines, clementines, or oranges

1 head garlic, halved

1 red Thai bird's eye chile (optional), chopped

¼ cup (20 g) chopped fresh rosemary

¼ cup (9 g) chopped fresh sage

4 sprigs fresh thyme, leaves picked

1 tablespoon black peppercorns

Extra-virgin olive oil

Kosher salt and freshly ground black pepper

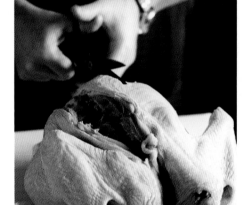

Remove the neck and giblets from the turkey cavity and discard the liver. Flip the turkey upside down so the breast is on your cutting board. Using heavy-duty kitchen shears, cut along both sides of the backbone to remove it. Cautiously but firmly open up the bird a little so it lies flatter, and set it on the board skin-side up.

In a large bowl, combine the citrus, garlic, chile, herbs, and peppercorns. Pour a generous amount of olive oil over the ingredients. Squeeze everything together with your hands, breaking up the citrus, to blend all of the flavors.

Place the turkey on a large platter and season generously on both sides with salt and pepper. Pour the marinade over the top. Rub onto both sides to make sure the whole turkey is coated. Cover with plastic wrap and refrigerate for at least 2 hours or overnight.

Remove the turkey from the refrigerator about 30 minutes before you are ready to smoke it.

SET UP THE SMOKER
Preheat a smoker to 225° to 250°F (110° to 120°C); see the instructions on page 16.

Add the turkey directly to the smoker rack and smoke until the juices run clear and the internal temperature of the thigh is 165°F (74°C), 4 to 5 hours total. Baste occasionally with the olive oil–citrus mixture as it cooks.

Remove the turkey and set aside, covered with foil, for at least 15 to 30 minutes before carving. Serve with your favorite gravy and side dishes.

SMOKED PRIME RIB

SERVES 8 TO 10

Another holiday favorite, this recipe has followed me from my Food Network days through all of my restaurants—it's simply that good. The prep is simple and incorporates all of the traditional flavors that make prime rib so great, from horseradish to fresh rosemary. Smoking the roast adds an extra element that you won't traditionally find, but I promise it's worth getting outside on a cold winter day to make this happen. Serve this with the M&L Potato Puree (page 207) and any green vegetable side for a full meal.

One 4-bone rib rack (13 to 14 pounds/6 to 6.5 kg)

5 cloves garlic, smashed, peeled, and minced

¼ cup (60 ml) prepared horseradish

2 tablespoons Dijon mustard

2 sprigs rosemary, needles picked

8 sprigs thyme, leaves picked

½ cup (69 g) kosher salt

¼ cup (28 g) fresh cracked black pepper

½ cup (120 ml) extra-virgin olive oil

PREP THE RIB RACK

Place the rib rack on a tray and pat completely dry with a paper towel. Place all the other ingredients into a bowl and mix well. Rub the rib rack with the mixture to create an even coat all over the roast. Set aside.

SET UP THE SMOKER

Preheat a smoker to 250°F (120°C); see the instructions on page 16.

COOK THE BEEF

Place the rib rack on the center of the smoker with the bone side on the grates and the meat side up. Close the lid and cook the rack for about 4 hours or until an internal temperature of 110°F (43°C) is reached.

SEAR THE BEEF

If you're using a ceramic, charcoal, or kettle smoker, remove the rack from the grates and open the air vents all the way. This will get the grill really hot at about 450°F (232°C). Place the rib rack back onto the grill for 30 to 45 minutes to get a nice crust on the outside and cook until an internal temperature of 128°F (53°C) is reached. Remove the rack from the grill and let rest for 20 minutes before carving. If you're using an electric or offset smoker, you'll need to finish this in an oven. Preheat to 450°F (232°C) and cook for 30 to 45 minutes to get your crust and reach your final temperature.

SMOKED PORK LOIN WITH APPLE-BRAISED CABBAGE

SERVES 8

Pork, apples, cabbage—there's no better trio when it comes to this protein. This is a dish that feels decidedly Midwestern—the blend of German heritage with American technique. The pork is coated in a wet rub and smoked (and braised) together with the cabbage mixture, the flavors all blending as they cook. You have a whole meal in one dish here, though it would be great alongside some hearty potatoes as well. We like to use Honeycrisp or Fuji apples, which add some sweetness but hold their shape well.

For the pork

½ cup (120 ml) Dijon mustard

¼ cup (60 ml) honey

2 tablespoons apple cider

1 tablespoon caraway seeds

1 tablespoon cumin seeds, toasted and crushed

Kosher salt and freshly ground black pepper

1 pork loin (3½ pounds/1.6 kg)

Fresh thyme sprigs

For the braised cabbage

1 head red cabbage, shredded

2 apples, cored and cut into ¼-inch (6 mm) slices

½ red onion, thinly sliced

½ cup (120 ml) apple cider

½ cup (120 ml) chicken broth

1 stick (4 ounces/115 g) unsalted butter, melted

2 tablespoons apple cider vinegar

¼ cup (50 g) sugar

2 bay leaves

2 teaspoons caraway seeds

2 teaspoons kosher salt

1 teaspoon freshly ground black pepper

PREPARE THE PORK

In a large bowl, mix together the mustard, honey, cider, caraway seeds, and toasted cumin seeds. Season generously with salt and pepper. Place the pork loin into the bowl and rub the mixture all over the pork. Cover and refrigerate overnight.

SET UP THE SMOKER

Preheat a smoker to 225° to 250°F (110° to 120°C); see the instructions on page 16. Remove the pork from the refrigerator to take the chill off while the smoker heats up.

PREPARE THE CABBAGE

In a large bowl, mix all of the braised cabbage ingredients together and spread into the bottom of a roasting pan. Place the rubbed pork on top, down the center of the pan, and cover the pork with a few thyme sprigs. Cover with aluminum foil.

Place the whole covered pan into the smoker. Cook until it reaches an internal temperature of 140°F (60°C), about 3 hours, checking occasionally to make sure there is enough liquid in the bottom of the pan (add more broth if necessary). Stir the cabbage around each time you check and baste the pork. Once wilted (about 2 hours in), remove the foil and continue cooking, basting a few more times.

Season the cabbage to taste and slice the pork into steaks. Serve everything together.

COWBOY
COOKING

ONE OF THESE YEARS, WHEN I SLOW DOWN AND HAVE A FEW MONTHS TO MYSELF, MY LONG-TIME DREAM IS TO HIT THE OPEN ROAD ON MY MOTORCYCLE. I'll do what I've taken to calling in my head "the great Western loop"—a 2,000-mile journey that starts in California and goes up and around the entire western half of the United States and back again. I'll meet up with chef friends who love to ride (this is something we talk about when we meet up at charity events, food festivals, and the like) and connect with others as I roll through their cities and sample their cuisine. Each day, when we've had enough on the bikes, we'll stop and set up camp under the stars, breaking out our portable grills or building a fire in order to get dinner going. The food in this chapter is what I imagine us cooking—cast-iron pots of stew nestled into firewood, breakfast skillets with just a few key ingredients, hearty chili and grilled jalapeño corn bread. My dreams might feel a little out of reach for most (or even me right now), but this kind of cooking is perfect for any weekend camping trip, backyard firepit, or portable beach barbecue. The only thing required? Some overhead stars.

PORK CHILE VERDE

SERVES 6 TO 8

The name of this stew comes directly from the ingredients inside—deep green and vibrant poblano chiles, punchy tomatillos, and spicy jalapeños—all grilled until charred and blistered and pureed with fresh green herbs. The whole stew can cook in a cast-iron pot on the grill until falling-apart tender. Set up a garnish station and let everyone top as desired—try to get a mix of crunchy, creamy, and cooling elements.

5 poblano chiles

2 pounds (910 g) tomatillos, stems and husks removed

3 jalapeños, plus more for garnish

2 yellow onions, sliced

2 heads garlic, tops removed

1 bunch fresh cilantro

½ cup pumpkin seeds

Juice of 2 limes

Kosher salt and freshly ground black pepper

3 pounds (1.4 kg) boneless pork shoulder, cut into large cubes

2 tablespoons extra-virgin olive oil

For serving

Sour cream

Sliced avocado

Fresh cilantro

Minced white onion

Grilled lime halves (see Grilled Citrus Garnish, page 21)

SET UP THE GRILL

Preheat a charcoal or gas grill to medium-high heat, and set it up with two zones: a hot side and cold (less hot) side, for direct and indirect cooking. (See method, page 15.) You want the temperature to hover around 400°F (205°C).

Place the poblanos, tomatillos, jalapeños (including the ones for garnish), onion slices, and garlic heads on the hot side of the grill. Cook until softened and charred, turning often, 8 to 10 minutes. Remove the stems from the chiles and place everything (just 3 jalapeños, saving the rest for garnish) into a high-powered blender. Add the cilantro, pumpkin seeds, and lime juice and puree until smooth. Season the green sauce to taste with salt and pepper.

Heat a large cast-iron pot on the hot side of the grill. Season the pork well with salt and pepper. Add the oil to the pot and when shimmering and starting to smoke, sear the pork on all sides until browned, 5 to 6 minutes total. Move the pot to the cooler side of the grill and pour the green sauce over the pork. Cover the pot and cook until the pork is very tender, 2½ to 3 hours. You will need to maintain the heat of the grill if using charcoal. Season to taste.

TO SERVE

Garnish with sour cream, avocado, cilantro, minced onion, reserved charred jalapeños, and grilled lime.

BIRRIA TACOS

SERVES 6

Birria, a traditional Mexican stewed meat dish originating in the state of Jalisco, has swept the Bay Area (and well beyond) in recent years, and we were all too excited to make our own version for the grill. What makes this so spectacular is the braising liquid (or jus) that you get after cooking the meat. Both the tortillas preassembly and the finished tacos get dipped in the vibrant red broth, which takes the melt-in-your-mouth shredded beef tacos to the next level. This recipe is one of those totally worth it "events" as opposed to a thrown-together dinner, though it can all be prepared ahead of time and assembled at the last minute.

For the wet rub

¼ cup (60 ml) extra-virgin olive oil

1 tablespoon garlic powder

1 tablespoon ground cumin

1 tablespoon ground coriander

1 tablespoon smoked paprika

1 tablespoon dried oregano

1½ tablespoons kosher salt

½ tablespoon freshly ground black pepper

For the beef

2 pounds (910 g) beef chuck, beef shoulder, or beef short ribs, boneless, cut into 2-inch (5 cm) chunks

For the beef braise

¼ cup (60 ml) extra-virgin olive oil

2 yellow onions, thinly sliced

6 cloves garlic, thinly sliced

1 jalapeño, thinly sliced

2 tablespoons tomato paste

2 tablespoons smoked paprika

4 dried guajillo chiles, seeded and stemmed

2 quarts (2 L) beef broth

For the tacos

Extra-virgin olive oil, for the griddle

10 to 12 (6-inch/15 cm) corn tortillas

8 ounces (225 g) mozzarella cheese or Oaxacan queso, sliced

1 yellow onion, minced

½ bunch fresh cilantro, roughly chopped

1 to 2 lemons or limes, sliced

SET UP THE GRILL

Preheat a charcoal or gas grill to medium-high heat, and set it up with two zones: a hot side and cold (less hot) side, for direct and indirect cooking. (See method, page 15.) You want the temperature to hover around 400°F (205°C).

MAKE THE WET RUB

In a bowl, mix together all the ingredients.

PREPARE THE BEEF

Add the beef to the bowl of wet rub and toss well to coat. Place the beef directly on the hot side of the grill and sear until some color forms and the surface begins to darken, turning to ensure even cooking, about 1 minute per side.

MAKE THE BEEF BRAISE

While you are searing the beef, place a Dutch oven over the hot side of the grill with the olive oil. Once the oil is smoking and shimmering, add the onions, garlic, and jalapeño and sauté until translucent, about 2 minutes. Stir in the tomato paste, smoked paprika, and guajillo chiles and continue to cook, stirring, until everything is evenly incorporated.

Add the grilled beef and broth to the Dutch oven and stir well. Cover the pot and move the Dutch oven to the cooler side of the grill. Cook for 2 hours, stirring occasionally. You will need to maintain the heat of the grill if using charcoal.

Uncover after 2 hours and cook until the meat is softened and falling apart, about 1 more hour.

Drain the liquid (the jus) from the beef and onions, reserving the jus. Shred the beef.

Return the jus to the grill (or move inside to a stovetop) and cook over medium heat to reduce for about 30 minutes. At this point

you can cool the shredded beef and jus and save for a later time to serve if you wish.

MAKE THE TACOS

When ready to make the tacos, have the warmed jus close to the grill. Place a cast-iron flattop griddle onto the grill over medium-high heat. Place a couple tablespoons of oil onto the griddle. Working one to two at a time, dip each tortilla in the jus and put directly on the griddle. Cook for about 30 seconds, then flip tortillas. Place a small amount of the beef mixture into the tortilla with some of the cheese. Fold in half. Once crisp, flip the taco over and cook for 1 to 2 more minutes. Once fully caramelized and the taco is hot all the way through, it is ready to serve. Repeat to make all the tacos.

Stir the minced onion and chopped cilantro into the hot jus mixture. Serve alongside the tacos with slices of fresh lemon or lime, instructing diners to dip the tacos into the jus.

COWBOY BEEF CHILI

SERVES 6 TO 8

I love to tinker with old recipes of mine, but every so often I find one that hits just perfectly. Such is the case with this old cowboy beef chili, which I ran on Food Network while filming *Tyler's Ultimate*. In my opinion, it truly remains to this day the ultimate Texas chili. Tightened with masa harina, it's made with a mix of bold Mexican chiles and beef shoulder (as opposed to ground beef), which cooks low and slow and falls apart into a tender, meaty stew. It definitely has a little kick, but you can tame that with lots of cooling toppings.

3 tablespoons extra-virgin olive oil

3 pounds (1.4 kg) beef shoulder, cut into large cubes

Kosher salt and freshly ground black pepper

2 tablespoons ancho chile powder

1 tablespoon ground coriander

1 tablespoon ground cumin

1 tablespoon sweet paprika

1 tablespoon dried oregano

¼ teaspoon ground cinnamon

2 onions, diced

10 cloves garlic, peeled and halved

3 canned chipotle peppers in adobo sauce, chopped

1 jalapeño, seeded and chopped

2 tablespoons tomato paste

1 teaspoon sugar

2 quarts (2 L) beef broth, plus more as needed

1 (28-ounce/794 g) can whole peeled tomatoes, crushed by hand

½ cup (65 g) masa harina

For serving

Shredded white cheddar cheese

Minced chives

Sour cream

Lime wedges

SET UP THE GRILL

Preheat a charcoal or gas grill to medium-high heat, and set it up with two zones: a hot side and cold (less hot) side, for direct and indirect cooking. (See method, page 15.) You want the temperature to hover around 400°F (205°C). While the grill is heating, place a large cast-iron or grill-safe pot on the hot side of the grill.

Add the olive oil to the pot. Season the beef with salt and black pepper. When the oil is very hot but not smoking, add the beef and cook, without stirring, until one side of the beef browns, 3 to 4 minutes. Stir and continue to brown the meat until all sides have color on them. You will need to do this in two or three batches so you have enough room to brown all the meat evenly. While the last batch is browning and it has about 1½ minutes left, stir in the ancho powder, coriander, cumin, paprika, oregano, and cinnamon. Return all the beef to the pot.

Meanwhile, in a food processor or blender, puree the onions, garlic, chipotle peppers, jalapeño, tomato paste, and sugar.

Add the onion-chipotle puree to the beef in the pot. Add enough broth to cover by 1 inch (2.5 cm) and add the tomatoes with their liquid. Bring to a boil and skim off any foam that rises to the surface. Move the pot to the cooler side of the grill. Let cook until the meat is fork-tender and comes apart with no resistance, about 2 hours. As it cooks down, add more broth if necessary, and continue to add coals or adjust the temp of the grill to keep it consistent.

Stir in the masa harina and bring back to a simmer for about 2 minutes. Take a potato masher and mash the chili so the meat comes apart in shreds. Season with salt and pepper to taste.

TO SERVE

Garnish each serving with the shredded cheddar, chives, sour cream, and lime wedges.

GRILLED JALAPEÑO CORN BREAD

MAKES ABOUT 12 MUFFINS

Spicy and slightly sweet, this is the perfect accompaniment to both the Pork Chile Verde (page 169) and the Cowboy Beef Chili (page 172)—or any other meaty stew you're putting together. It's also great on its own. I have fun mini corn on the cob cast-iron molds, so I couldn't resist making these in them. Obviously, I don't expect that to be part of your kitchen collection—this will be just as good "grill-baked" in a cast-iron skillet or regular muffin tins.

For the corn bread muffins

1 cup (125 g) all-purpose flour

1 cup (180 g) cornmeal

¼ cup (55 g) packed brown sugar

1 teaspoon baking powder

½ teaspoon baking soda

2 teaspoons kosher salt

4 tablespoons (60 g) unsalted butter, melted

¼ cup (60 ml) canola oil

1 cup (240 ml) buttermilk

¼ cup (60 ml) honey

2 large eggs

½ cup (70 g) corn kernels, fresh or thawed frozen

1 jalapeño, sliced

For the salted honey butter

2 sticks (8 ounces/225 g) unsalted butter, at room temperature

⅓ cup (75 ml) honey, plus more for garnish

½ teaspoon kosher salt

Flaky sea salt, for garnish

SET UP THE GRILL

Preheat a charcoal or gas grill to medium-high heat, and set it up with two zones: a hot side and cold (less hot) side, for direct and indirect cooking. (See method, page 15.) You want the temperature to hover around 400°F (205°C).

MAKE THE CORN BREAD MUFFINS

In a bowl, whisk together the flour, cornmeal, brown sugar, baking powder, baking soda, and salt. In a separate bowl, whisk together the melted butter, canola oil, buttermilk, honey, and eggs until smooth.

Pour the wet mixture into the dry mixture and whisk until fully combined and smooth. Fold in the corn and sliced jalapeño.

GRILL-BAKE THE CORN BREAD

Grease a muffin tin with cooking spray to evenly coat. Fill each cup of the muffin tin about three-quarters of the way with the batter.

Place the filled muffin tin on the cooler side of the grill and close the lid. Bake for 8 minutes, then rotate the pan 180 degrees (front to back) and bake until a cake tester or toothpick inserted into the center of the muffin comes out clean, about an additional 8 minutes.

Let cool off slightly before serving.

MEANWHILE, MAKE THE SALTED HONEY BUTTER

While the muffins are cooking, in a bowl, combine the butter, honey, and salt and mix well. Serve garnished with a little extra honey and some flaky sea salt.

Serve the muffins with the salted honey butter.

SEAFOOD AND CHICKEN PAELLA

SERVES 6 TO 8

I had to include this labor-intensive but totally worth-it paella, one of those showstopper dishes that's so fun to bring to a table full of guests. Loaded with everything from chicken and chorizo to lobster and clams, the whole rice dish is topped with a fragrant lemon-saffron aioli. The key to good paella is getting the rice cooked just right, with a layer of crispy rice on the bottom. Setting the pan right on the grill helps achieve that, and once I have the rice where I want it, I'll "decorate it" with everything else.

For the chicken

1 pound (455 g) boneless, skinless chicken thighs, halved

1 tablespoon pimentón (Spanish smoked paprika)

1 teaspoon dried oregano

1 teaspoon kosher salt

1 teaspoon extra-virgin olive oil

For the paella

8 cups (2 L) low-sodium chicken broth

A large pinch of saffron threads

5 teaspoons kosher salt

1 yellow onion, diced

8 cloves garlic, peeled

1 fennel bulb, diced

¼ cup (60 ml) extra-virgin olive oil

8 ounces (225 g) Spanish hard-cured chorizo, diced

2 tablespoons tomato paste

1 cup (240 ml) white wine

2 cups (455 g) Spanish bomba rice

For the seafood

3 lobster tails, halved lengthwise

½ pound (225 g) peeled and deveined shrimp (about 10)

½ pound (225 g) steamer clams (about 12)

½ pound (225 g) mussels (about 10), cleaned

2 teaspoons extra-virgin olive oil

1 teaspoon dried oregano

2 teaspoons pimentón

Grated zest and juice of 1 lemon

MARINATE THE CHICKEN

Place the chicken in a small bowl and mix well with the pimentón, oregano, salt, and olive oil. Set aside to marinate for at least 20 minutes.

SET UP THE GRILL

Preheat a charcoal or gas grill to medium heat with a target temperature of 350°F (175°C). If using charcoal, light your charcoal and spread it out into an even layer on the bottom of the grill with about 1 inch of space in between all the coals.

MAKE THE PAELLA

In a large pot on the stove or direct heat on the grill, combine the chicken broth, saffron, and salt and heat over low heat. Don't bring it to a boil, but get it hot and set aside.

In a food processor, combine the onion, garlic, and fennel and process it down until it makes a pulp-like consistency, about 1 minute. Set the sofrito aside.

Place a paella pan or 12- to 13-inch (30 to 33 cm) grill-safe skillet on the grill grates. Add the olive oil to the pan and let it get hot, just until the oil begins to shimmer and smoke. Add the sofrito and chorizo to the pan and sauté until it starts to fry in the oil, about 5 minutes. Add the tomato paste and mix well until it is evenly distributed. Add the white wine and let cook and reduce for 2 minutes. Add the rice and stir well. Add the warmed chicken broth and stir together until everything is in an even layer in the pan. Do not stir after this. Bring to a simmer and cook with the lid of the grill down for 30 minutes, rotating the pan every 10 minutes, or until the grains of rice are fully cooked. Cover with foil and set aside.

recipe continues

ingredients continue

For the lemon-saffron aioli

1 large egg

2 egg yolks

1 clove garlic, peeled

Grated zest and juice of 1 lemon

1 teaspoon Dijon mustard

Pinch of saffron threads

1½ teaspoons kosher salt

1½ cups (360 ml) blended oil (olive and
     canola or vegetable, etc.)

For serving

Lemons, for garnish

Fresh green herbs, for garnish

COOK THE SEAFOOD AND CHICKEN

Light some more charcoal in the grill and set it up with two zones: a hot side and cold (less hot) side, for direct and indirect cooking. (See method, page 15.) You want the temperature to hover around 400°F (205°C). Or set your gas grill accordingly.

Place all of the seafood into a bowl and add the olive oil, oregano, pimentón, and lemon zest.

Place the marinated chicken thighs on the hot side of the grill until you have some good grill marks, about 3 minutes.

Flip the chicken over and transfer to the cooler side of the grill. At the same time, place the seafood into a grill basket and place on the hot side of the grill. Cover the grill and cook the chicken and seafood for about 5 minutes, giving the seafood a few stirs in the basket to cook everything evenly. Cook the chicken to an internal temperature of 155°F (68°C) and until the clams and mussels open and the lobster and shrimp are firm and opaque in color.

Remove the chicken and seafood from the grill, squeeze the lemon juice over the seafood, and arrange in a fun design on the top of the paella rice.

MAKE THE LEMON-SAFFRON AIOLI

In a blender, combine the whole egg, egg yolks, garlic, lemon zest, lemon juice, mustard, saffron, and salt and mix on medium speed. Once fully combined, with the machine running, start to drizzle in the oil to fully emulsify the aioli.

TO SERVE

Dollop the aioli over the top of the paella and garnish with lemons and green herbs. Serve immediately.

BEER CAN CHICKEN WITH SALSA VERDE

SERVES 4

Beer can chicken is all about the steam. Typically, when you're grilling a whole chicken, you're relying on dry heat to cook the bird from the outside in. Placing a beer can in the cavity—or, if you want to get fancy, a roaster designed to hold the chicken upright with liquid in a cup underneath—ensures that the chicken will steam from the inside as it simultaneously cooks from the outside. It produces a crazy-tender and juicy end result. We love to serve this one with all the Mexican garnishes to make for a festive main course.

For the chicken

1 whole chicken (3½ to 5 pounds/1.5 to 2.5 kg)

2 tablespoons extra-virgin olive oil

1½ tablespoons ground cumin

1½ tablespoons ground coriander

1½ tablespoons smoked paprika

1½ tablespoons kosher salt

½ tablespoon freshly ground black pepper

6 ounces (180 ml) Mexican lager (half a can of beer), still in the open can

For the salsa verde

¾ pound (340 g) tomatillos, peeled and quartered

½ yellow onion, sliced

1 serrano chile, sliced

1 poblano chile, sliced

½ tablespoon ground cumin

½ tablespoon ground coriander

3 cloves garlic

2 tablespoons extra-virgin olive oil

1 teaspoon kosher salt, plus more to taste

½ teaspoon freshly ground black pepper

1 cup (240 ml) chicken stock

½ bunch fresh cilantro

Juice of 2 limes

For the garnishes

Fresh cilantro

Cotija cheese

Grilled limes (see Grilled Citrus Garnish, page 21)

Green onions, sliced thin

SET UP THE GRILL

Preheat a charcoal or gas grill to medium-high heat, and set it up with two zones: a hot side and cold (less hot) side, for direct and indirect cooking. (See method, page 15.) You want the temperature to hover around 400°F (205°C).

PREP THE CHICKEN

Pat the chicken completely dry using paper towels. Gently rub the olive oil all over the chicken. Mix the cumin, coriander, smoked paprika, salt, and pepper in a bowl. Generously season the chicken with the spice mixture until it is fully coated in an even layer.

Place the bottom cavity of the chicken over the top of the beer can and place in the center of a cast-iron or heavy-bottomed small pan that will fit on your grill.

PREP THE SALSA VERDE

Combine the cut tomatillos, onions, serrano and poblano chiles, cumin, coriander, garlic, olive oil, salt, and pepper in a bowl and mix well. Place the vegetables around the chicken in the pan.

Cook the chicken and salsa: Place the pan of chicken and vegetables onto the cold side of the grill and close the lid. Cook the chicken for 45 to 60 minutes total, stopping halfway through to rotate the pan 180 degrees and add the chicken stock. When finished, the chicken should have an internal temperature of about 155°F (68°C). Remove the chicken and vegetables from the grill and let the chicken rest for about 10 minutes before slicing it.

FINISH THE DISH

Place all the vegetables into a blender with the fresh cilantro and lime juice. Puree until smooth, and add salt to taste. Place the salsa on the bottom of a large platter. Once the chicken has rested, cut into quarters and place over the top of the salsa. Garnish with cilantro, Cotija cheese, grilled limes, and green onions. Serve hot.

DENVER BREAKFAST SKILLET

SERVES 4

This is about as easy as a camping breakfast gets. Diced peppers, onions, and ham are cooked in a cast-iron skillet over the flames, then are topped with cracked eggs and Monterey Jack cheese. The whole thing cooks super quickly and is enough to both feed a crowd and keep you full until lunchtime. Though traditionally this is the blend for a "Denver" omelet, feel free to play with ingredients if you want to add something else to the pan...this is your chance to use up whatever is left over from your camping dinner the night before.

3 tablespoons extra-virgin olive oil

1 small onion, finely diced

1 red bell pepper, finely diced

2 Anaheim or 1 poblano or green bell pepper, finely diced

1 ham steak (8 ounces/225 g), finely diced

4 large eggs

½ cup (55 g) shredded Monterey Jack cheese or shredded melting cheese of choice

Kosher salt and freshly ground black pepper

For serving

Minced fresh chives

Minced fresh parsley

Grilled bread

SET UP THE GRILL

Preheat a gas or charcoal grill (or build a live firepit with a grate over the top for cooking) to medium-high heat, with a target temperature of 400°F (205°C). Warm a cast-iron skillet over the fire.

Once the skillet is hot, add the olive oil, onion, bell pepper, and Anaheim peppers and sauté until the onion is becoming translucent, 3 to 4 minutes.

Add the ham and stir to combine. Cook until the ham gets a bit of color on it, 2 to 3 minutes more. Using a spoon, make 4 depressions in the vegetable and ham mixture. Crack the eggs into each of the 4 indents, then sprinkle the Monterey Jack on top. Season the whole thing with salt and pepper.

Close the lid of the grill and cook until the cheese has melted and the eggs are cooked to your preferred doneness, 3 to 5 minutes. If you're cooking on a firepit, cover the pot to finish cooking.

TO SERVE

Garnish with fresh chives and parsley and serve hot with grilled bread.

CAMPFIRE POTATOES WITH TOMATOES, BACON, AND BLUE CHEESE

SERVES 6 TO 8

Behind the scenes, we started calling these "wedge salad potatoes," since they get topped with all of our favorite steakhouse garnishes—bacon, tomato, onions, blue cheese. But really, that's just an easy way to spruce up this easy one-pot side dish, where marble potatoes are cooked down in a garlicky, buttery broth that thickens into a glaze as the potatoes soften. Serve it alongside any of the steaks or chops for a fun—and hearty—steakhouse experience.

For the potatoes

6 tablespoons (90 g) unsalted butter

3 pounds (1.4 kg) marble potatoes

Kosher salt and freshly ground black pepper

6 cloves garlic, minced

5 cups (1.2 L) low-sodium chicken broth

For the garnishes

3 to 4 slices bacon, cooked and cut into lardons

¾ cup (100 g) crumbled blue cheese

Crème fraîche

Pickled Red Onions (page 95)

Grilled cherry tomatoes (see Note)

Minced fresh chives

SET UP THE GRILL

Preheat a charcoal or gas grill to medium-high heat, and set it up with two zones: a hot side and cold (less hot) side, for direct and indirect cooking. (See method, page 15.) You want the temperature to hover around 400°F (205°C). Place a large cast-iron skillet on top of the grates to heat as the grill warms up.

COOK THE POTATOES

When the skillet is hot, add the butter to melt. Add the potatoes and toss to coat. Season generously with salt and pepper. Add the garlic and 3½ cups (840 ml) of the broth and move the skillet to the cooler side of the grill. Close the lid and let the potatoes cook down, basting occasionally, until cooked through and the liquid has mostly evaporated, adding more broth as needed for the potatoes to cook. You'll likely end up needing close to 5 cups.

Remove the potatoes from the grill and serve hot, topped with bacon lardons, blue cheese, dollops of crème fraîche, pickled onions, grilled tomatoes, and minced chives.

Note: To grill the tomatoes, look for whole cherry tomatoes right on the vine, which you can drop directly onto the hot side of the grill grates as the potatoes finish cooking. Once they have slightly charred and started to burst, they're finished. If you can't find whole tomatoes on the vine, place the tomatoes either in a cast-iron skillet on the grates or in an aluminum foil packet (not too tightly sealed).

SIDES

WE ALWAYS SAY AT THANKSGIVING THAT YOU'RE EITHER A TURKEY PERSON OR A SIDES PERSON, BUT I DON'T THINK IT APPLIES JUST TO THAT HOLIDAY.

Toss me a spoon and a deli container of my mother-in-law Marge's potato salad any day of the week, and that's a full meal for me. In many ways, this is where I really love to get creative, especially on the grill. It's so easy to get stuck in a rut when you're cooking sides outside, and to stick to the basics like grilled rafts of zucchini or pepper, fat rounds of onion, or corn on the cob. Not that any of that is bad, but how about trying the grilled ratatouille instead, where everything stays whole in a grill basket to make for a stunning visual; or get a pot of stewed beans going over the coals. Sear a peach and toast some bread for a seasonal panzanella; or stick some sweet potatoes in a smoker while you finish a pork shoulder. To be fair, not all of the sides in the chapter to come are cooked on the grill (no reason to add a heated element to a perfectly crisp and creamy coleslaw or mess with my long-perfected Miller & Lux steakhouse sides), but everything here has a partner (or twelve) alongside other recipes in the book. They're all pretty darn good on their own, too.

GRILLED RATATOUILLE

SERVES 4

Real talk : Traditional ratatouille is one of the most annoying dishes to make. The chopped vegetables are sautéed individually and later layered in so that everything cooks evenly, and the finished product is . . . good, but not earth-shattering. This grilled side, however, is anything but traditional. Break out the grill basket and fill it with different cuts—halved baby eggplant, thick-sliced zucchini and summer squash, whole tomatoes and onions— that can be prepped in minutes and will slowly cook over the grill without falling apart. You'll never go back.

5 medium tomatoes, left whole

½ yellow onion, cut into rings

1 zucchini, cut into ½-inch (1.3 cm) slices

1 yellow squash, cut into 1-inch (2.5 cm) slices

1 Japanese eggplant, halved lengthwise

⅓ cup (75 ml) extra-virgin olive oil

Kosher salt and freshly ground black pepper

¾ cup (180 ml) pesto, for serving

Fresh basil, for garnish

SET UP THE GRILL

Preheat a charcoal or gas grill to medium-high heat with a target temperature of 400°F (205°C).

Toss all the vegetables into a bowl with the olive oil and season to taste with salt and pepper. Mix until everything is nicely coated. Arrange the vegetables into the grill basket so they are spread out and there is some room for everything to cook evenly.

Place the basket over the grill, close the lid, and cook for about 10 minutes. Stir or flip the basket over and repeat until everything is nicely browned, slightly charred, soft, and the tomatoes have just burst open, another 10 minutes.

Serve the ratatouille on a platter, or straight from the basket for a rustic feel, topped with dollops of the pesto and garnished with fresh basil.

GRILLED PEACH PANZANELLA

SERVES 4 TO 6

The pure essence of summer, this tomato and bread salad is studded with juicy peaches, chile heat, and crunchy cucumbers and onions and is topped with oozing torn burrata. I love it because having bread and vegetables together means that all you need is a grilled meat alongside—we love this with the Reverse-Seared Grilled Chicken Base Recipe (page 87)—to make it a full meal. It's great to use day-old bread, which soaks up the tomato juice like a sponge; but even if you're using fresh, a quick turn on the grill will help dry it out while it crisps.

½ loaf ciabatta bread, halved horizontally

2 medium peaches, halved and pitted

10 tablespoons (60 ml) extra-virgin olive oil, divided, plus more for drizzling

Kosher salt

½ English cucumber, sliced

½ small red onion, sliced

2 medium tomatoes, cut into large chunks

1 Fresno chile, sliced

¼ cup (60 ml) red wine vinegar

½ teaspoon freshly ground black pepper

¼ bunch fresh basil leaves, torn, plus more for garnish

2 balls burrata cheese

Flaky sea salt, for garnish

SET UP THE GRILL

Preheat a charcoal or gas grill to medium-high heat with a target temperature of 400°F (205°C).

Brush the bread and peaches with 4 tablespoons olive oil and season the bread with salt. Place the bread and peaches directly on the grates. Grill the bread for 1 to 2 minutes per side until it is nice and toasty. Some edges will appear blackened, which is okay. Grill the peaches 4 to 5 minutes total, flipping once two-thirds of the way through. Cut the bread and peaches into 1-inch (2.5 cm) pieces and set aside.

Meanwhile, in a bowl, combine the cucumber, red onion, tomatoes, and chile. Mix the grilled bread and peaches in with this mixture and add the vinegar, 6 tablespoons olive oil, 1 teaspoon salt, the pepper, and fresh basil. Mix thoroughly and set aside to marinate for at least 20 minutes or up to 4 hours.

When ready to serve, place the salad on a platter or in a shallow bowl. Tear the burrata into 8 total pieces and arrange on top of the salad. Garnish with some basil, a drizzle of olive oil, and some flaky sea salt.

MARGE'S POTATO SALAD

SERVES 4 TO 6

If you dug around on the Internet—or through my other cookbooks—you'd find this exact recipe printed a time or two. There's a very good reason for that. This is my mother-in-law Marge's potato salad and, in my opinion, the ultimate version. Though I'm always playing with and adjusting old recipes, this one is just as it should be—creamy, briny, crunchy, earthy. It's everything you want for a summer side dish and it goes with just about every main course possible, from brisket to barbecue chicken. How could I leave it out?

2 pounds (910 g) small Yukon Gold
    potatoes

2 large eggs

Kosher salt

½ bunch green onions, sliced

2 tablespoons drained capers

1 cup (240 ml) mayonnaise

¼ cup (60 ml) Dijon mustard

¼ cup (55 g) finely chopped dill pickle

¼ cup (60 ml) pickle juice

1 small red onion, chopped

2 tablespoons chopped fresh flat-leaf
    parsley

Juice of ½ lemon

Freshly ground black pepper

Set up a bowl of ice and water. Place the potatoes and eggs in a saucepan of cold salted water. Bring to a simmer. After 12 minutes, remove the eggs with a slotted spoon and plunge them into the ice water to cool. Continue cooking the potatoes until tender, 3 to 4 minutes longer. Drain the potatoes in a colander and let them cool.

Set aside some green onions and capers for garnish. In a bowl large enough to hold the potatoes, stir together the mayonnaise, mustard, pickles, pickle juice, onion, remaining green onions and capers, the parsley, and lemon juice.

Peel the cooled eggs and grate them into the bowl. Peel the cooled potatoes with a paring knife. Cut the potatoes into chunks and toss with the dressing to coat. Season with salt and pepper to taste.

Garnish with the reserved green onions and capers. Serve immediately or refrigerate for up to 4 days.

CREAMY CABBAGE, LIME, AND CILANTRO COLESLAW

SERVES 4 TO 6

You can find hundreds of thousands of creamy coleslaw recipes anywhere you search, but this one has a more nontraditional spin. Here, lime zest and cilantro give it a Tex-Mex vibe, which means it's as good on tacos or served with the Reverse-Seared Pollo Asado (page 95) as it is topping a BBQ Turkey Meatball Slider (page 118). Take it to the next level by adding sliced serrano if you want some chile heat.

½ cup (120 ml) sour cream

½ cup (120 ml) mayonnaise

¼ cup (60 ml) extra-virgin olive oil

1½ tablespoons sugar

Grated zest and juice of 2 limes, plus more to taste

Kosher salt and freshly ground black pepper

1 medium head savoy cabbage, shredded or thinly sliced

4 green onions, thinly sliced on the bias

½ bunch fresh cilantro, minced

In a bowl, combine the sour cream, mayonnaise, olive oil, sugar, lime zest, and lime juice. Season with salt and pepper.

In a large bowl, toss together the cabbage, green onions, and cilantro. Pour the dressing over the cabbage mixture and toss to combine. Taste and add more salt, pepper, or lime juice if needed. Serve cold.

RED BEANS AND RICE

SERVES 4 TO 6

This is campfire comfort at its best, but you can make these anywhere there's good heat—on a pot over a pile of logs or on your stovetop. The andouille adds a little kick, but we like to up the ante at the end with a vinegar-based hot sauce; adjust to your liking. If you want to make these vegetarian, omit the sausage and ham hock and add smoked paprika for a little bit of that campfire flavor.

For the beans

¼ cup (60 ml) extra-virgin olive oil

4 andouille sausages

2 stalks celery, diced

1 medium yellow onion, diced

1 green bell pepper, diced

1 pound (455 g) dried red kidney beans,
    soaked overnight and drained

1 ham hock

4 cloves garlic, peeled

3 bay leaves

3 sprigs fresh thyme

4 cups (960 ml) chicken stock

Kosher salt and freshly ground black pepper

¼ bunch fresh parsley, minced

For the rice

2 cups (370 g) long-grain white rice

2 cloves garlic, smashed and peeled

4 tablespoons (60 g) unsalted butter

2 teaspoons kosher salt

Chopped green onions, for garnish

SET UP THE GRILL

Preheat a charcoal or gas grill to medium-high heat, and set it up with two zones: a hot side and cold (less hot) side, for direct and indirect cooking. (See method, page 15.) You want the temperature to hover around 400°F (205°C). Place a cast-iron or grill-safe pot over the hot side of the grill as it heats up.

MAKE THE BEANS

When the pot is hot, add the oil and andouille sausage and cook, stirring, until the sausage is browned, 3 to 4 minutes. Add the celery, onion, and bell pepper and continue to sauté until the vegetables are softened, another 3 to 4 minutes. Add the beans, ham hock, garlic, bay leaves, thyme, and chicken stock. Cover the pot and move to the cooler side of the grill. Simmer, stirring occasionally, until beans are soft, about 1 hour.

Remove the ham hock and bay leaves and season to taste generously with salt and pepper. Stir in the parsley.

MEANWHILE, MAKE THE RICE

When the beans are almost done, place the rice and 3 cups (720 ml) water in a small pot with the garlic, butter, and salt. Bring to a boil over direct heat on the grill. Once boiling, reduce the heat to low, move the pot to the cool side of the grill, and cover the pot with a lid. Cook until the liquid is absorbed, about 15 minutes. Once cooked, remove the lid and fluff the rice with a fork. You can also make the rice on the stove using the same timing.

Serve the beans and rice together, garnished with chopped green onions.

BROCCOLI RICE PILAF

SERVES 4 TO 6

I love this broccoli rice pilaf, another of those two-sides-in-one dishes, because it's both super kid-friendly and fun to make—fresh broccoli is grated straight into the hot, cooked ginger rice when it comes off the stove, which means it cooks just enough in the heat to take the raw edge out of the vegetable but still have a nice bite to it. Serve this with the Teriyaki Cedar Plank Salmon (page 116) or as a base for the Vietnamese-Style Beef Skewers (page 38) for a little something extra.

For the rice pilaf

2 cups (370 g) long-grain white rice

4 cups (960 ml) chicken stock

4 tablespoons (60 g) unsalted butter

1 knob fresh ginger, peeled and roughly chopped

2 cloves garlic, roughly chopped

1 tablespoon soy sauce

1 tablespoon rice wine vinegar

1 teaspoon sesame oil

2 teaspoons kosher salt

For the broccoli

1 head broccoli, grated

4 green onions, sliced

MAKE THE RICE PILAF

Place all the ingredients in a medium saucepot. Place the pot over medium-high heat and once the rice begins to boil, cover the pot and reduce the heat to low. Simmer for 15 minutes. When no liquid remains and the rice is cooked through, use a fork to fluff the rice.

MAKE THE BROCCOLI

Once the rice is cooked, place the grated broccoli and half of the green onions into the pot and fold into the hot rice.

Spoon the broccoli rice pilaf onto a large serving platter and garnish with the rest of the green onions. Serve hot.

TWICE-SMOKED MAPLE SWEET POTATOES

SERVES 8

You'll find this recipe paired with the Smoked Pork Shoulder (page 151), but it's also a perfect side dish to just about anything else in the book. The sweet jewel-toned yams pick up the nuanced notes of maple, coriander, orange zest, and Parmesan cheese that flavor the filling, along with a hit of smokiness from the wood chips. Of course, you can just as easily bake these or cook them straight on the grill, which will allow them to finish much faster. These would be especially good with the Reverse-Seared Grilled Chicken with Barbecue Sauce (page 91) or Santa Maria-Style Tri-Tip (page 139).

8 small to medium sweet potatoes, poked
    with a fork
2 sticks (8 ounces/225 g) unsalted butter,
    at room temperature
3 tablespoons maple syrup
1 teaspoon ground coriander
Grated zest of 1 orange
½ cup (50 g) grated Parmesan cheese,
    plus more for garnish
2 tablespoons minced chives, plus more for
    garnish
1½ tablespoons kosher salt

SET UP THE SMOKER
Preheat a smoker to 250°F (120°C); see instructions on page 16.

Place the poked potatoes into the smoker. Cook until tender, about 2 hours.

While the potatoes are cooking, in a medium bowl, stir together the butter, maple syrup, ground coriander, orange zest, Parmesan, chives, and salt.

Halve the potatoes and scrape the flesh out into a bowl (hold on to the skins). Mix with the compound butter while still hot. Spoon the flesh back into the potato skins and place back in the smoker for another 30 minutes. When finished, garnish with more Parmesan and minced chives.

GRILLED TRUFFLE MACARONI AND CHEESE

SERVES 6

Some version of this macaroni and cheese has followed me through most of my career, whether it was made with cheddar cheese on the Food Network or served alongside my famous fried chicken at my San Francisco flagship restaurant, Wayfare Tavern. This one gets an elevated spin from the addition of truffle paste and earthy, tangy Dry Jack cheese alongside young Monterey Jack. Most of this is made inside, so if you want to finish it there, no need to do the last step on the grill—that said, if the grill is still hot from cooking your main course, it makes for a fun flourish at the end.

For the garlic bread crumbs

3 cloves garlic, minced

1 cup (80 g) panko bread crumbs

2 tablespoons extra-virgin olive oil

Kosher salt

¼ cup (25 g) grated Parmesan cheese

For the mac and cheese

Kosher salt

4 tablespoons (60 g) unsalted butter

¼ cup (30 g) all-purpose flour

2 cups (480 ml) heavy cream

2 cups (480 ml) whole milk

1 tablespoon truffle paste

2 cloves garlic, minced

5 sprigs fresh thyme

2 bay leaves

2 teaspoons kosher salt

½ teaspoon freshly ground black pepper

½ pound (225 g) Dry Jack cheese, shredded

1 pound (455 g) small pasta shapes, such as
    elbow macaroni, fusilli, or torchio

Extra-virgin olive oil

½ pound (225 g) Monterey Jack cheese,
    shredded

3 to 4 tablespoons minced fresh chives, for
    garnish

MAKE THE GARLIC BREAD CRUMBS

In a small bowl, mix the garlic and panko together until well combined. Add the olive oil, season with salt, and mix well until the panko has all evenly soaked up the olive oil. In a medium sauté pan, toast the panko mixture over medium heat, tossing frequently to evenly cook until golden brown, 3 to 4 minutes. Remove the bread crumbs from the pan and return to the bowl. Toss the Parmesan into the hot mixture to melt and coat evenly. Set aside.

SET UP THE GRILL

Preheat a charcoal or gas grill to medium heat with a target temperature of 350°F (175°C).

MAKE THE MAC AND CHEESE

Bring a large pot of heavily salted water to a boil over high heat on the stove for the pasta.

Meanwhile, in a separate pot, melt the butter over medium heat. Add the flour to make a roux, stirring well so that it cooks evenly and turns golden blond. Whisk in the cream and milk a little bit at a time, so there are no lumps. Add the truffle paste, garlic, thyme sprigs, and bay leaves, stirring well to combine. Simmer over medium heat, stirring occasionally to prevent the bottom of the pot from scorching, until it thickens, about 10 minutes. Season the béchamel with the salt and pepper. Discard the thyme sprigs and bay leaves. Stir in the Dry Jack cheese until smooth and silky. Let sit while you cook the pasta.

Once the pasta water is boiling, add the pasta and cook according to the package directions. Drain. Coat with a little olive oil after it's been drained to keep the pasta from sticking.

Mix the cheese sauce with the cooked pasta. Immediately add the Monterey Jack cheese and mix well, so that the heat and motion melt and stretch the cheese. Transfer to a grill-safe 9 by 13-inch (23 by 33 cm) baking dish and top with the bread crumbs.

GRILL THE MAC AND CHEESE

Place the baking dish on the grill. Close the lid and cook until the bread crumbs are golden brown and the dish is bubbling, about 10 minutes. If you want to finish this inside, put it in the oven at 400°F (205°C) for 7 to 10 minutes.

To finish, drizzle with extra-virgin olive oil and sprinkle with the chives.

GRILLED ASPARAGUS WITH MISO SESAME SAUCE

SERVES 8

Throwing some asparagus on the grill is about as easy a vegetable side as you can do when making other things. It cooks in minutes, and the stalks are great with some char and crispy edges. A miso sesame sauce to finish (which can be made ahead of time) takes it from basic to bold and allows the versatile vegetable to fit better into a more Asian-themed menu. To keep these from falling through the grates, cook them in a grill basket, which will make the whole experience even more stress-free.

For the miso sesame sauce

2 cloves garlic, peeled

1 shallot, roughly chopped

3 tablespoons tamari

1 tablespoon mirin

2 tablespoons sherry vinegar

2 tablespoons rice vinegar

1 tablespoon light miso paste

1 tablespoon light brown sugar

½ cup (120 ml) vegetable oil

2 tablespoons sesame oil

2 tablespoons black sesame seeds

For the asparagus

2 bunches asparagus, trimmed

¼ cup (60 ml) sesame oil

Kosher salt and freshly ground black pepper

MAKE THE MISO SESAME SAUCE

In a blender, combine the garlic, shallot, tamari, mirin, both vinegars, the miso, and brown sugar and puree until smooth. With the blender running on medium, slowly drizzle in the vegetable oil. Transfer to a bowl or jar and stir in the sesame oil and sesame seeds. This can be made well ahead.

SET UP THE GRILL

Preheat a charcoal or gas grill to medium-high heat with a target temperature of 400°F (205°C).

GRILL THE ASPARAGUS

Toss the asparagus with the sesame oil and season to taste with salt and pepper. Arrange in a grill basket, place on the grill, and cook, turning and shaking once or twice, until softened and slightly charred, 10 to 12 minutes.

Serve the asparagus warm, drizzled with the miso sesame sauce.

M&L POTATO PUREE

SERVES 4

This isn't a "grilled side" per se, but our Miller & Lux potato puree may just
be the best version of mashed potatoes you'll ever make. It's a side dish that's
as versatile (especially with grilled meats) as it is creamy and delicious. It's
obviously our first choice next to our signature steaks and is a great partner
to other sides like the Double-Creamed Kale with Crispy Shallots (page 210)
or Mushrooms Bourguignon (page 208). If you don't have a ricer, you can easily
place the drained potatoes into the pot with the cream and mash them with a
whisk or potato masher, or use an electric hand mixer to incorporate them.

2 pounds (910 g) Yukon Gold or other
   yellow potatoes

4 cloves garlic, peeled

Kosher salt and freshly ground black
   pepper

1¼ cups (300 ml) heavy cream

4 tablespoons (57 g) unsalted butter

1 bunch fresh chives, minced, for garnish

Peel and roughly chop the potatoes. Add them along with the
garlic to a pot of cold salted water. Bring to a simmer and cook the
potatoes until tender, 10 to 12 minutes. Once the potatoes are fully
cooked, drain and set aside.

In a sauté pan, combine the cream and butter and bring to a
simmer over medium-low heat. Place the potatoes into a ricer and
squeeze into the pan with the cream and butter. Using a whisk,
gently fold everything together. Season with salt and pepper
to taste.

Serve the potatoes warm, garnished with minced chives.

MUSHROOMS BOURGUIGNON

SERVES 4

I think of this dish more as a good "smothering" side, as it's pretty close to perfect smeared on top of any grilled steak. The richness of the bourguignon would add another layer of luxury to a special-occasion meal. It's a hearty enough side dish that it can stand on its own as a main course served with something creamy—like Parmesan polenta or potato puree—and can also be a vegetarian entrée if you sub vegetable broth for beef.

6 tablespoons (90 g) unsalted butter

2 tablespoons extra-virgin olive oil

1 pound (455 g) brown button mushrooms

1 pound (455 g) pearl onions, blanched and peeled

2 sprigs fresh thyme

2 sprigs fresh rosemary

3 carrots, thinly sliced

5 cloves garlic, sliced

1 tablespoon tomato paste

1 tablespoon all-purpose flour

1 cup (240 ml) red wine

1 cup (240 ml) beef broth

Kosher salt and freshly ground black pepper

1 bunch fresh chives, minced, for garnish

Fresh flat-leaf parsley, leaves picked, for garnish

In a large sauté pan, heat 4 tablespoons (60 g) of the butter and olive oil over medium-high heat. Once the butter is starting to brown, add the mushrooms, pearl onions, thyme, and rosemary and sauté until the onions and mushrooms have browned, about 5 minutes.

Remove the mushrooms, onions, and herbs from the pan and place on a tray or plate lined with a paper towel and set aside. You can discard the herbs at this point. It's okay if some of the residual fat stays in the pan; you can use this for the sauce.

Return the sauté pan used to cook the mushrooms to the stove over medium heat. Add the remaining 2 tablespoons (30 g) butter to the pan. Once the butter is melted, add the carrots and garlic and sauté for 5 minutes, stirring constantly.

Stir in the tomato paste and flour until the contents thicken. Gently stir in the wine to deglaze the pan and simmer for 1 to 2 minutes, to allow the alcohol to cook off. Add the beef broth and bring to a simmer. Return the mushrooms and onions to the pan and simmer, stirring occasionally, until thickened, about 15 minutes. Taste and season with salt and pepper.

Spoon the mushrooms into a serving dish and garnish with minced chives and parsley leaves. Serve hot.

DOUBLE-CREAMED KALE
WITH CRISPY SHALLOTS

SERVES 4

A California version of the steakhouse classic, this side dish gets its vibrant green color and deep, nuanced earthiness from pureeing the cooked spinach. This is one of our more popular side dishes at Miller & Lux, one that I'd be destroyed for if I were to take it off the menu. And truly, there would never be a need—it's pretty great just as is and holds up well to serve the next day.

For the greens

Kosher salt

¾ pound (340 g) spinach, cleaned

¾ pound (340 g) lacinato kale, tough ribs
   removed

For the crispy shallots

2 large or 3 small shallots, peeled

1 cup (125 g) all-purpose flour

Kosher salt and freshly ground black pepper

Grapeseed or canola oil, for deep-frying

For the béchamel

½ tablespoon extra-virgin olive oil

2 tablespoons (30 g) unsalted butter

1 yellow onion, minced

1 fennel bulb, minced

2 cloves garlic, sliced

Kosher salt and freshly ground black pepper

2 tablespoons all-purpose flour

½ teaspoon grated nutmeg

¼ cup (60 ml) Herbsaint or Pernod

1 cup (240 ml) whole milk

To finish

2 tablespoons (30 g) unsalted butter

¾ cup (70 g) freshly grated Parmesan cheese

BLANCH THE GREENS

Bring a large pot of generously salted water to a boil. Add the spinach, and as soon as it's wilted and tender, 1 to 2 minutes, drain and run under cold water. When the spinach is cool enough to handle, squeeze out any excess water. If you have used whole spinach with long stems, roughly chop it. You should have about 1½ cups (340 g) of chopped spinach. Repeat this process with the kale and set aside. The kale will need to cook about 2 minutes longer than the spinach.

MAKE THE CRISPY SHALLOTS

Thinly slice the shallots into disks and break the disks into rings with your hands. Rinse the shallot rings with warm water a couple of times to wash some of the juices off, which will prevent them from cooking too quickly and burning. On a plate, season the flour with a bit of salt and pepper and toss the shallot rings in the flour.

Pour 1 inch (2.5 cm) of grapeseed or canola oil into a large, deep sauté pan or Dutch oven and heat to 325°F (165°C). Line a plate with paper towels.

Add a handful of shallot rings to the oil, making sure they have room to move. Fry in the oil until golden brown, 3 to 4 minutes. Transfer to the paper towels to drain. If desired, keep them warm in a 200°F (90°C) oven.

MAKE THE BÉCHAMEL

Heat a large sauté pan over medium heat. Add the olive oil and butter and when melted, add the onion, fennel, garlic, and a few pinches of salt. Cook until the onion is translucent but not browned, about 3 minutes. Add the flour and nutmeg and stir to coat. When the flour has brought the onion mixture together, add the Herbsaint and bring to a boil. Let it reduce by half, then stir in the milk to make a béchamel. Season to taste with salt and pepper. Cook at a low simmer until the sauce thickens to the point where it coats the back of a spoon and drawing your finger down the spoon leaves a clear line.

Pour the béchamel into a blender with the spinach. Blend until completely smooth and neon green. Pour the green béchamel into a pan and fold in the kale. Heat, stirring, and season with salt and pepper. Finish by stirring in the butter and Parmesan.

Transfer the creamed kale to a serving dish, and top with the crispy shallots.

SWEETS

WHEN YOU THINK ABOUT DESSERTS ON THE GRILL, NOT A WHOLE LOT COMES TO MIND. Rings of pineapple, perhaps, with crosshatch grill marks. Peach halves charred and served with vanilla ice cream. And maybe, if you're getting really creative, slices of pound cake kissed on the grates. But when you think of your grill as an oven, the options become endless. Find a few grill-safe pans, and anything you can bake inside can be put in an indirect heat situation under the lid of your grill. In this chapter, we played with cookie skillets and upside-down cakes, cobblers and tarts, and even came up with a riff on the childhood classic s'mores, done nacho-style. Prep dessert ahead of time and take advantage while the grill is still hot from dinner to finish it off outside. You'll get just enough smoky flavor to perfectly cap off a multicourse grilled feast, with fun endings to satisfy any sweet tooth.

MATT'S BERRY BISCUIT COBBLER

SERVES 6

My corporate chef, Matt Masera, was an insanely good pastry chef back in the day (and still is), so I love to go to him first when I'm thinking about dessert. This is one of his longtime specialties, and it couldn't be easier to make. The rustic hominess of the dish lends itself perfectly to the end of a cookout meal—scooped into bowls and topped with ice cream, it's truly one of those desserts that appeals to all ages and can be tailored with any fruit to fit the seasons.

For the cobbler filling

2 pounds (910 g) mixed berries

¾ cup (165 g) light brown sugar

¾ cup (150 g) granulated sugar

2½ tablespoons potato or tapioca starch

Grated zest and juice of ½ lemon

2 teaspoons kosher salt

1½ teaspoons vanilla extract

Pinch of ground cinnamon

For the biscuit top

2 cups (250 g) all-purpose flour

1 tablespoon sugar

2 teaspoons baking powder

1 teaspoon kosher salt

1½ cups (360 ml) heavy cream

For serving

Vanilla ice cream

Fresh mint, for garnish

SET UP THE GRILL

Preheat a charcoal or gas grill to medium heat, and set it up with two zones: a hot side and cold (less hot) side, for direct and indirect cooking. (See method, page 15.) You want the temperature to hover around 350°F (175°C). If too hot, close the air vents and cool the heat down.

MAKE THE COBBLER FILLING

In a large bowl, toss the berries with both sugars, the starch, lemon zest, lemon juice, salt, vanilla, and cinnamon. Place in a large cast-iron skillet or grill-safe baking dish and press into an even layer. Set aside.

MAKE THE BISCUIT TOP

In a stand mixer fitted with the paddle, combine the flour, sugar, baking powder, and salt and gently mix together on low speed. Slowly pour the cream into the mixer and blend just until fully combined.

Using a portion scoop or large spoon, place 6 large dollops of biscuits across the top of the berries, spaced evenly. Place the dish onto the cooler side of the grill and close the lid. Cook for 15 minutes. Rotate the baking dish front to back and cook until the biscuits are golden brown and the fruit is bubbling and thick, another 10 minutes.

Serve warm with vanilla ice cream and garnish with fresh mint leaves.

GRILLED STRAWBERRY UPSIDE-DOWN CAKE

SERVES 6 TO 8

This started out as a strawberry shortcake, which felt like a necessary addition to any good grill book. But as often happens, a little playing around with the format led to this super-fun upside-down cake. Placing whole strawberries in the bottom of the pan means that when it's flipped, the batter creates cavernous little tunnels around the fruit, perfect for catching drips of soft whipped cream. It's a stunner to look at and even better to eat.

For the pound cake

1 stick (4 ounces/115 g) unsalted butter, at room temperature

2 tablespoons vegetable oil

1½ cups (300 g) sugar

1 teaspoon kosher salt

3 large eggs

2¼ cups (280 g) all-purpose flour

1 tablespoon baking powder

¾ cup (180 ml) buttermilk

1 tablespoon vanilla extract

8 to 10 large whole strawberries, hulled

For the whipped cream

2 cups (480 ml) heavy cream, cold

1 tablespoon sugar

½ teaspoon kosher salt

For serving

Fresh whole strawberries, for garnish

Fresh mint sprigs, for garnish

MAKE THE POUND CAKE BATTER

In a stand mixer fitted with the paddle, combine the butter, oil, sugar, and salt and beat until all the butter has creamed together, making a paste-like consistency. Add the eggs one at a time, beating well after each addition, until fully incorporated. Beat in the flour and baking powder, then beat in the buttermilk and vanilla. Mix until just smooth, taking care not to overmix.

SET UP THE GRILL

Preheat a charcoal or gas grill to medium heat, and set it up with two zones: a hot side and cold (less hot) side, for direct and indirect cooking. (See method, page 15.) You want the temperature to hover around 350°F (175°C). If too hot, close the air vents and cool the heat down.

Grease a grill-safe 9 by 5-inch (23 by 12 cm) loaf pan. Line the bottom of the loaf pan evenly with the whole strawberries and pour batter over the top.

Place the loaf pan on the grill, close the lid, and cook until a toothpick inserted into the center comes out clean, about 45 minutes.

MEANWHILE, MAKE THE WHIPPED CREAM

In a bowl, whisk the cream, sugar, and salt until soft peaks form (or do this in a stand mixer with the whisk attachment).

TO SERVE

When the cake has cooled slightly, invert onto a platter. Top with big dollops of whipped cream, fresh strawberries, and sprigs of fresh mint.

LEMON POLENTA POUND CAKE WITH WHIPPED CREAM, BLUEBERRIES, AND BASIL

SERVES 8

This bright cake has Italian roots, using hearty cornmeal as a base, and it also has that traditional Italian not-too-sweet thing going on. It then gets balanced with juicy blueberries and whipped cream. We made ours in a Bundt pan, but you can cook it in any grill-safe cake pan.

For the cake

1 cup (125 g) all-purpose flour

1 cup (120 g) polenta cornmeal

½ cup (110 g) light brown sugar

1 teaspoon baking powder

½ teaspoon baking soda

2 teaspoons kosher salt

Grated zest of 1 lemon

¼ cup (60 ml) canola oil

1 cup (240 ml) buttermilk

¼ cup (60 ml) honey

2 large eggs

1 teaspoon vanilla extract

4 tablespoons (60 g) unsalted butter, melted

For the glaze

1½ cups (340 g) powdered sugar

2 tablespoons fresh lemon juice

Pinch of kosher salt

For the whipped cream

2 cups (480 ml) heavy cream

3 tablespoons sugar

1 teaspoon vanilla extract

Pinch of kosher salt

Garnishes

Fresh blueberries

Fresh basil leaves

Lemon zest

SET UP THE GRILL

Preheat a charcoal or gas grill to medium-high heat, and set it up with two zones: a hot side and cold (less hot) side, for direct and indirect cooking. (See method, page 15.) You want the temperature to hover around 375°F (190°C). If too hot, close the air vents and cool the heat down.

Grease a grill-safe Bundt pan, 9-inch (23 cm) cake pan, or baking dish.

MAKE THE CAKE

In a bowl, combine the flour, cornmeal, brown sugar, baking powder, baking soda, salt, and lemon zest.

In another bowl, combine the oil, buttermilk, honey, eggs, and vanilla and whisk the mixture together while drizzling the melted butter into it. Combine the wet ingredients with the dry ingredients and let sit for 10 minutes to allow the polenta to soften a bit before baking.

Pour the batter into the cake pan and place onto the cooler side of the grill. Close the lid and bake the cake for 15 to 20 minutes, depending on the size of the pan—longer for the Bundt pan. Rotate the pan front to back and bake until a toothpick inserted into the center of the cake comes out clean, another 12 to 20 minutes. Let cool before unmolding.

MAKE THE GLAZE

In a small bowl, stir together the sugar, lemon juice, 1 tablespoon water, and salt until smooth. Drizzle over the cooled cake.

MAKE THE WHIPPED CREAM

In a stand mixer fitted with a whisk, combine the cream, sugar, vanilla, and salt. Whisk until soft peaks form.

If serving the cake whole, spoon the whipped cream into the center (directly in the hole if you used a Bundt pan), and garnish with blueberries, fresh basil, and lemon zest. Otherwise, slice the cake into wedges and place a piece onto each plate. Top with a dollop of the whipped cream, fresh blueberries, basil, and lemon zest.

BOURBON CARAMEL APPLE STREUSEL

SERVES 6

At the very last minute when we were developing this recipe, we threw in some bourbon, and that instantly took it to the next level. The whole thing bubbles into a fragrant, apple-studded caramel on the grill and is the perfect dessert for a fall menu. Use crisp, sturdy apples here like Fuji or Honeycrisp, which aren't mealy and will hold up well as they bake.

For the streusel topping

2 sticks (8 ounces/225 g) unsalted butter, melted

1¼ cups (275 g) packed light brown sugar

1¾ cups (220 g) all-purpose flour

½ cup (45 g) rolled oats

1 teaspoon kosher salt

½ teaspoon vanilla extract

For the apples

2 sticks (8 ounces/225 g) plus 2 tablespoons (30 g) unsalted butter

1½ cups (330 g) brown sugar

1⅓ cups (265 g) granulated sugar

¼ cup (60 ml) bourbon

4 pounds (1.8 kg) apples, peeled and diced

¼ cup (30 g) cornstarch

2 teaspoons kosher salt

½ tablespoon ground cinnamon

½ teaspoon ground cloves

Juice of ½ lemon

Vanilla ice cream, for serving

MAKE THE STREUSEL

Preheat the oven to 350°F (175°C).

In a bowl, stir together the melted butter, brown sugar, flour, oats, salt, and vanilla. Spread out onto a sheet pan and bake for 5 minutes. Let cool and set aside.

SET UP THE GRILL

Preheat a charcoal or gas grill to medium heat, and set it up with two zones: a hot side and cold (less hot) side, for direct and indirect cooking. (See method, page 15.) You want the temperature to hover around 350°F (175°C). If too hot, close the air vents and cool the heat down.

MAKE THE APPLES

In a Dutch oven or cast-iron skillet, combine the butter and both sugars and melt over the hot side of the grill. Cook, stirring occasionally, until they emulsify and turn into a toffee-like consistency. When it reaches the color and consistency of toffee, stir in the bourbon.

In a large bowl, toss the apples with the cornstarch, salt, and spices. Add the apples to the toffee mixture and cook until thick and translucent, about 5 minutes. Stir in the lemon juice.

Top the apples with the streusel mixture and move the whole pan to the cooler side of the grill. Cover the grill and bake until the top is crisp and the apple mixture is thickened and bubbling, about 30 minutes, rotating the pan a couple of times to keep the heat even.

Serve warm, with ice cream.

HONEY PEAR GALETTE WITH WALNUTS AND GORGONZOLA

MAKES 1 GALETTE; SERVES 6

As much a tart as a galette, this earthy, wintery dessert may not be for everyone—I know some shy away from blue cheese on their sweets—but I'd tell those people they'd be missing out. I decided to swap out regular almond marzipan for a walnut version here, which adds a sharper, more complex base layer to pair with the pears and cheese. For rustic presentation purposes, I love to leave the peel, stem, and seeds right in the pear slices. It's easy enough to eat around the woodier parts, but if you'd rather not, peel and core the fruit.

½ recipe Galette Dough (recipe follows)

All-purpose flour, for rolling

For the walnut marzipan

2 cups (200 g) walnuts

¼ cup (30 g) powdered sugar

6 tablespoons (85 g) light brown sugar

3 large eggs

¼ teaspoon ground nutmeg

¼ teaspoon ground cinnamon

⅛ teaspoon ground allspice

¾ teaspoon kosher salt

Grated zest of 1 small orange or tangerine

For the topping

3 to 4 pears, cut into lengthwise slices
 ½ inch (1.3 cm) thick

1 egg yolk

2 tablespoons heavy cream

Turbinado sugar, for sprinkling

⅓ cup (45 g) crumbled Gorgonzola cheese

For serving

Chopped fresh thyme

Chopped toasted walnuts

Honey, for drizzling

Make the dough and refrigerate as directed. Let the dough come to room temp before rolling out.

Roll the dough out onto a sheet of floured parchment into a rectangle slightly larger than 9 by 13 inches (23 by 33 cm). Gently press the whole thing, parchment and dough, into a 9 by 13-inch (23 by 33 cm) grill-safe pan and crimp the edges. Refrigerate the pan with the dough while making the filling.

MAKE THE WALNUT MARZIPAN

In a food processor or high-powered blender, mix all of the marzipan ingredients together until well blended. It should feel like a thick but easily workable paste.

SET UP THE GRILL

Preheat a charcoal or gas grill to medium heat, and set it up with two zones: a hot side and cold (less hot) side, for direct and indirect cooking. (See method, page 15.) You want the temperature to hover around 350°F (175°C). If too hot, close the air vents and cool the heat down. Place a pizza stone over the cooler side of the grill and let it heat up as the grill heats.

TOP THE GALETTE

Spread the walnut marzipan evenly into the bottom of the galette crust. Arrange the pears in a single layer artfully over the marzipan. Mix the egg yolk and cream together and gently brush over the dough and filling. Sprinkle with turbinado sugar and evenly disperse the Gorgonzola over the top.

Place the galette onto the pizza stone and cook until the galette turns golden brown, about 45 minutes, rotating the pan front to back every 15 minutes.

TO SERVE

Garnish with chopped thyme, chopped walnuts, and a drizzle of honey.

GALETTE DOUGH

MAKES ENOUGH DOUGH FOR TWO 9 BY 13-INCH (23 BY 33 CM) GALETTES

2½ cups (315 g) all-purpose flour

1 tablespoon sugar

2 teaspoons kosher salt

2 sticks (8 ounces/225 g) unsalted butter

In a food processor, combine the flour, sugar, salt, butter, and ¼ cup (60 ml) ice water and blend until large crumbles are formed. Remove from the food processor and place on a work surface. Bring together into a solid dough ball and wrap in plastic wrap. Refrigerate for at least 1 hour.

Remove the dough from the refrigerator and divide into 2 equal portions. Freeze the portion you are not using and let the other portion of dough come to room temp before rolling out.

CARAMEL KETTLE CORN

SERVES 4

As the coals are cooling and the embers are dying out on the grill or campfire, this is a great sweet snack or dessert to finish off a camping experience. Shaking the pan while it cooks is super important, so the sugars don't burn. When you hit it just right, the caramel cools into a shattering crust that makes each popped kernel burst with the sweet and salty flavor that makes kettle corn so addicting.

¼ cup (60 ml) vegetable oil

4 tablespoons (57 g) unsalted butter

2¼ teaspoons kosher salt

½ cup (106 g) popcorn kernels

¼ teaspoon ground cinnamon

½ cup (100 g) sugar

1 teaspoon vanilla extract

SET UP THE GRILL

Preheat a charcoal or gas grill to high heat with a target temperature of 500°F (260°C). Place a large cast-iron Dutch oven with a lid on the grill.

When the pot is hot, add the vegetable oil, butter, and salt. Right before the butter begins to brown, add the popcorn and cinnamon. Stir the kernels around the pot until they start popping. As soon as they start, add the sugar and vanilla to the pot and cover with the lid. Shake the pan to make sure the sugar and corn mix inside the pan. While the corn is popping, shake the pan vigorously every 15 seconds to prevent burning on the bottom. Once the popping starts to slow down, remove from the heat and uncover. Pour the mixture out onto a sheet pan or other flat surface immediately and spread the popcorn out. Let cool before serving.

S'MACHOS

SERVES 6 TO 8

Truly, there may not be a more easily thrown-together recipe in this book than this decadent dessert, which riffs nacho-style on the childhood classic. After you've made dinner on the grill and need a little something sweet, assemble this sheet pan of s'more-style nachos and go to town. Aside from the must-haves of graham crackers, chocolate (this is the only place I'll ever use Hershey's), and marshmallows, which is really all you need, you can use any other toppings you have lying around the pantry—here we went with pretzels for a little salt, berries for color, a drizzle of chocolate ganache, and cacao nibs for crunch.

12 graham crackers (full double sheets)

4 Hershey's bars (1.55 ounces/43 g each)

1 cup (64 g) mini salted pretzels

1½ cups (70 g) mini marshmallows

2 ounces (57 g) bittersweet chocolate, chopped

½ cup (120 ml) heavy cream, warmed

2 cups (250 g) raspberries or other berries of choice

2 tablespoons cacao nibs

SET UP THE GRILL

Preheat a charcoal or gas grill to medium heat, and set it up with two zones: a hot side and cold (less hot) side, for direct and indirect cooking. (See method, page 15.) You want the temperature to hover around 350°F (175°C). If too hot, close the air the vents and cool the heat down.

Line a grill-safe quarter-sheet pan (9 by 13 inches/23 by 33 cm) with parchment paper. Break up the graham crackers into shards and toss on the baking sheet with the broken-up chocolate bars, pretzels, and marshmallows.

Place the pan on the cooler side of the grill and close the lid. Bake until the chocolate is melted and the marshmallows are toasted, 18 to 20 minutes.

As the s'machos are ready to come off the grill, mix the chopped bittersweet chocolate and warm cream together until you have a smooth ganache.

Scatter berries over the top of the s'machos and drizzle with the ganache. Garnish with cacao nibs and serve immediately.

GLUTEN-FREE ROCKY ROAD BROWNIE BITES

MAKES 24 BROWNIE BITES

Dress up these bite-size chocolate brownies with any toppings you choose, though we love the marshmallow-walnut duo with a punch of dried cherries. The fact that the brownies are gluten-free is an extra bonus—they're made with sweet rice flour, which keeps the texture moist and light.

6 tablespoons (90 g) unsalted butter

8 ounces (225 g) bittersweet chocolate, chopped

3 large eggs

¼ cup (50 g) sugar

¼ cup (55 g) light brown sugar

½ teaspoon kosher salt

½ cup (80 g) mochiko or other sweet rice flour

1½ teaspoons vanilla extract

48 mini marshmallows

24 dried cherries (about ¼ cup/35 g)

¼ cup (30 g) chopped walnuts

In a small saucepan, melt the butter over medium-low heat. Once melted, add the chocolate and let that melt into the butter, stirring occasionally, until smooth. Cool the chocolate slightly.

While the chocolate is cooling, in a stand mixer fitted with the whisk, combine the eggs, both sugars, and salt and whisk on medium speed until light and frothy, 4 to 5 minutes. Whisk in the rice flour and vanilla. With the mixer running on low speed, slowly pour in the chocolate-butter mixture and whisk until combined.

SET UP THE GRILL

Preheat a charcoal or gas grill to medium-high heat, and set it up with two zones: a hot side and cold (less hot) side, for direct and indirect cooking. (See method, page 15.) You want the temperature to hover around 375°F (190°C) to 400°F (205°C). If too hot, close the air vents and cool the heat down.

Grease a grill-safe 24-cup mini muffin tin well with butter or cooking spray.

Divide the batter among the muffin cups. Top each with 2 marshmallows, 1 dried cherry, and a couple crumbles of walnut. Place on the cooler side of the grill and close the lid. Bake until the batter has cooked through and the marshmallows are toasted, 15 to 20 minutes.

Let cool slightly before turning out onto a wire rack. Serve warm or store in an airtight container until ready to serve.

TRES LECHES CAKE

SERVES 6 TO 8

Tres leches is a popular California dessert, due in large part to the Latin influence we have in this region. And that's a good thing, because this soaked cake—doused with three milks, as the name suggests—is, in my opinion, one of the best ways to finish a simple cake. This batter is the same as for the Grilled Strawberry Upside-Down Cake (page 217), which really shows its versatility. It's great just on its own, but sturdy enough to hold up to a liquid bath. Properly wrapped up, this will keep in the fridge for at least a few days.

For the cake

1 stick (4 ounces/115 g) unsalted butter, at room temperature
2 tablespoons vegetable oil
1½ cups (300 g) sugar
1 teaspoon kosher salt
3 large eggs
2¼ cups (280 g) all-purpose flour
1 tablespoon baking powder
¾ cup (180 ml) buttermilk
1 tablespoon vanilla extract

For the garnish

2 cups (400 g) granulated sugar
1 orange, thinly sliced

For the frosting

2 cups (480 ml) heavy cream
3 tablespoons granulated sugar
½ teaspoon kosher salt
½ teaspoon vanilla extract

For the soak and assembly

1 cup (240 ml) whole milk
1 can (14 ounces/397 g) sweetened condensed milk
1 can (12 ounces/354 ml) evaporated milk
Powdered sugar, for sprinkling
Ground cinnamon, for dusting

MAKE THE CAKE BATTER

In a stand mixer fitted with the paddle, combine the butter, oil, sugar, and salt and cream them together, making a paste-like consistency. Add the eggs one at a time, beating well after each addition. Beat in the flour and baking powder. Beat in the buttermilk and vanilla and mix until just smooth, taking care not to overmix.

SET UP THE GRILL

Preheat a charcoal or gas grill to medium heat, and set it up with two zones: a hot side and cold (less hot) side, for direct and indirect cooking. (See method, page 15.) You want the temperature to hover around 350°F (175°C). If too hot, close the air vents and cool the heat down.

Grease a grill-safe 9-inch (23 cm) cake pan.

Pour the batter into the pan and place over the cooler side of the grill. Bake until the center of the cake batter bounces back when pressed, about 45 minutes, rotating the pan front to back every 15 minutes.

MEANWHILE, MAKE THE GARNISH

While the cake is baking, in a saucepan, combine the sugar and 2 cups (480 ml) water and bring to a boil. Once the sugar is dissolved, take down to a simmer and add the orange slices. Simmer until the syrup has thickened and the oranges are softened and caramelized, 15 to 20 minutes.

MAKE THE FROSTING

In a bowl, with a whisk or hand mixer, whip together the cream, sugar, salt, and vanilla until soft peaks form.

When the cake is done, remove from the grill and cool completely before soaking.

SOAK AND ASSEMBLE THE CAKE

Remove the cake from the pan and place on a platter. Poke holes all across the top of it with a fork to help let steam off and allow the soak to set in better.

In a bowl, stir together the three milks and pour all over the top of the cake in small batches, allowing it to soak in completely before serving.

Spread the frosting all over the top of the cake. Top with the orange slices and sprinkle with powdered sugar and a light dusting of cinnamon.

GRILLED RICOTTA AND HONEY CHEESECAKE

SERVES 6 TO 8

I love this grilled cheesecake for its unusual but incredibly appealing flavor. Dairy tends to soak up flavors and aromas around it, so this base quickly picks up the smokiness from the grill. This recipe is custardy, so it cooks best in a water bath, which is actually great for the grill—while most would shy away from baking on the grates because of hot spots, the water bath is insurance for even cooking. We've given a berry sauce below, but finish it with any seasonal fruit or fruit sauce to make it a year-round dessert.

For the graham crust

2 cups (240 g) graham cracker crumbs

⅓ cup (65 g) granulated sugar

½ teaspoon kosher salt

1 stick (4 ounces/115 g) unsalted butter, melted

For the cheesecake

1½ pounds (680 g) cream cheese

¾ cup (150 g) granulated sugar

2 tablespoons cornstarch

1 teaspoon kosher salt

20 ounces (570 g) ricotta cheese

¼ cup (60 ml) honey

4 large eggs

1 teaspoon vanilla paste or extract

For the berry sauce

2 pounds (910 g) mixed berries, such as blackberry, raspberry, blueberry, strawberry

½ cup (100 g) granulated sugar

Juice of ½ lemon

1 teaspoon vanilla extract

For serving

Mixed fresh berries, for garnish

Powdered sugar, for dusting

Fresh mint, for garnish

MAKE THE CRUST

Preheat the oven to 325°F (165°C).

In a bowl, mix together the graham crumbs, granulated sugar, salt, and melted butter. Press the crumbs about ½ inch (1.3 cm) thick into the bottom of a 9-inch (23 cm) springform pan. Place the pan into the oven and bake for 10 minutes. Remove and let cool to room temperature.

SET UP THE GRILL

Preheat a charcoal or gas grill to medium heat, and set it up with two zones: a hot side and cold (less hot) side, for direct and indirect cooking. (See method, page 15.) You want the temperature to hover around 350°F (175°C). If too hot, close the air vents down and cool the heat down.

MAKE THE CHEESECAKE

In a stand mixer fitted with the paddle, beat the cream cheese until whipped and room temperature. In a small bowl, mix the granulated sugar, cornstarch, and salt together. Add to the cream cheese and mix until fully incorporated. Beat in the ricotta and honey, followed by the eggs and vanilla, beating until smooth.

Pour the batter over the graham cracker crust and place the pan into a larger, deep grill-safe pan. Pour hot water into the outer pan, halfway up the sides of the cheesecake pan. Cover the inner pan with foil and place on the cool side of the grill. Close the lid and bake until the cheesecake jiggles, about 1 hour 15 minutes.

MEANWHILE, MAKE THE BERRY SAUCE

In a saucepan, combine the berries, granulated sugar, lemon juice, and vanilla and bring to a simmer. Cook until the berries are softened and slightly thickened, 10 to 15 minutes. Puree the sauce and pass through a fine-mesh sieve. Let the cheesecake cool completely before serving.

Serve the cheesecake topped with the berry sauce and fresh berries. Dust with powdered sugar and garnish with fresh mint.

SKILLET CHOCOLATE CHUNK COOKIE

SERVES 8 TO 10

I used to consistently keep pre-portioned chocolate chip cookie dough in the freezer, so if we were having friends over, I could easily pull out as many as needed for fresh chocolate chip cookies. Now I'll try to plan ahead just enough to get some dough in the fridge that I can press into a round skillet and make a "pizzookie." There's nothing better than grabbing a spoon and tucking into this as it comes right off the grill, with just enough smoke flavor to make it interesting. Top it with vanilla ice cream and flaky sea salt and get messy.

2 cups (250 g) all-purpose flour

½ teaspoon baking soda

1½ teaspoons kosher salt

1 stick (4 ounces/115 g) unsalted butter, browned (see Note)

1 cup (225 g) lightly packed dark brown sugar

1 cup (200 g) granulated sugar

1 tablespoon pure vanilla extract

2 large eggs

¾ cup (125 g) white chocolate chips

¾ cup (130 g) bittersweet chocolate chunks

Flaky sea salt, to finish

Vanilla ice cream, for serving

SET UP THE GRILL

Preheat a charcoal or gas grill to medium-high heat with a target temperature of 400°F (205°C).

Grease a 12-inch (30 cm) cast-iron skillet.

Into a medium bowl, sift together the flour, baking soda, and salt.

In a stand mixer fitted with paddle, combine the browned butter, brown sugar, and granulated sugar and cream them together on medium speed until light and fluffy, 2 to 3 minutes. Scrape down the sides of the bowl with a rubber spatula. Beat in the vanilla and eggs. Gradually add the flour mixture to the butter-sugar mixture and continue to mix just until a smooth dough forms. Fold in the white chocolate chips and chocolate chunks by hand.

Press the cookie dough into the cast-iron skillet. Transfer to the grill, close the lid, and cook until just slightly gooey in the center and cooked throughout, 25 to 30 minutes.

Sprinkle flaky sea salt over the top, and serve warm with vanilla ice cream.

Note: To make browned butter, melt butter in a heavy-bottomed skillet over medium heat. The butter will start to foam up as it melts, and the foam will then subside. Stir occasionally as it continues to cook; the butter will brown quickly, so keep an eye on it. Once it has turned golden and smells nutty, it's done. Remove from the heat and immediately pour into a heatproof bowl.

RUBS, OILS, SAUCES, AND EXTRAS

IF YOU THINK OF THIS BOOK AS A TECHNIQUE-BASED ROADMAP, THIS MIGHT JUST BE THE MOST IMPORTANT CHAPTER. Learning what tools to use, how to fire up the grill—or smoker—and exactly how (and how long) to cook each different main ingredient is three-quarters of the battle. Once you've mastered that, you can move past exact recipes and play around with flavors. This chapter has everything you need to start and finish most dishes, from the rubs that add depth and nuance to smoked meat, to the sauces that elevate your food beyond just a seasoned piece of protein. Play around, get creative, and make these dishes your own— that's what takes you from a novice cook who follows exact recipes to a grill prodigy. Trust yourself and get some help from the recipes that follow. It will expand your repertoire tremendously.

REVERSE-SEAR DRY BRINE

MAKES ABOUT ½ CUP (120 G)

This is what we use to start most chicken dishes. Once you've dry-brined and slow-cooked your poultry, you can finish it in countless different directions (see pages 87 to 95). But this would also work well on pork chops or even a skirt or flank steak.

2 tablespoons fresh thyme leaves

2 tablespoons fresh rosemary leaves

Grated zest of 1 to 2 lemons

4 cloves garlic, grated on a Microplane

5 teaspoons kosher salt

1½ teaspoons sugar

1 teaspoon freshly ground black pepper

⅓ cup (75 ml) extra-virgin olive oil

In a medium bowl, stir together all of the ingredients until well blended. Use immediately.

BBQ SAUCE

MAKES ABOUT 2 CUPS (480 ML)

This has long been my go-to barbecue sauce. Spiced and sweet, we use it often—ribs, chicken, brisket, meatballs, you name it. You'd be smart to have a container of this in the fridge all summer long. It makes enough to have leftovers, and it will store well in an airtight jar or container for at least a couple of weeks.

1 slice bacon

1 bunch fresh thyme

2 tablespoons extra-virgin olive oil

½ yellow onion, diced

2 cloves garlic, sliced

2 cups (480 ml) ketchup

4 tablespoons brown sugar

¼ cup (60 ml) molasses

2 tablespoons red wine vinegar

1 tablespoon mustard powder

1 teaspoon ground cumin

1 teaspoon paprika or smoked paprika

Freshly ground black pepper

Wrap the bacon slice around the bunch of thyme and tie it together with a bit of cooking twine.

In a medium saucepan, heat the oil over medium heat. Place the bacon-wrapped thyme in the pan and cook until the bacon starts to get crispy, about 4 minutes. Add the onion and garlic to the bacon grease and sauté until they begin to caramelize, about 5 minutes.

Add the ketchup, brown sugar, molasses, vinegar, mustard powder, cumin, and paprika. Season with black pepper and mix well. Let come to a boil, reduce the heat, and simmer for 2 to 3 minutes. Discard the bacon-wrapped thyme.

GOCHUJANG HONEY LIME SAUCE

MAKES ¾ CUP (180 ML)

We use this on our wing recipe (page 34), but it can easily be used anytime to add a sweet and spicy note to grilled meats, shrimp, or even rice or noodle dishes.

   ½ cup (120 ml) gochujang (Korean chile paste)
   ¼ cup (60 ml) honey
   Juice of 1 lime

In a small bowl, whisk together the gochujang, honey, and lime until well mixed. Store in the refrigerator in an airtight container until ready to use.

KIMCHI RANCH

MAKES 1 CUP (240 ML)

Every so often we come up with something that feels a little revolutionary, and this spicy, briny ranch fell into that category. We developed it to go with Korean-style wings, but it's really just a fun take on a dressing that we already know goes with everything. You can just as easily put a bowl of this out for your crudités platter as you can for your wing dip.

   ¼ cup (60 ml) mayonnaise
   ¼ cup (60 ml) sour cream
   ½ cup (75 g) kimchi, drained, squeezed,
      and dried on paper towels
   ½ teaspoon garlic powder
   ½ teaspoon onion powder
   ½ teaspoon kosher salt

In a bowl, mix together the mayonnaise, sour cream, kimchi, garlic powder, onion powder, and salt. Refrigerate until ready to use.

SMOKER SPRITZ

MAKES 1 CUP (240 ML)

If you're going through the slow and steady process of using the smoker, you'll want to have a bottle of this on hand. It's a very simple blend of water and acid, but it keeps the meat on the smoker from drying out.

   ½ cup (120 ml) apple cider vinegar
   Juice of ½ lemon

Stir together ½ cup (120 ml) water, the vinegar, and lemon juice and pour into a spray bottle. Shake well.

FRESH HERB PESTO

MAKES 2½ TO 3 CUPS (600 TO 720 ML)

Our backyard herb garden is the inspiration for so many dishes and sauces that come out of the kitchen, but if there's one thing we make most using the bounty, it's probably this simple homemade pesto. This is one of those dishes that's so much better when you make it fresh rather than buying it from the store, and the effort is pretty minimal. Leftovers will freeze well. (I like to use the large cocktail ice cube trays for portioning it out.)

    1 bunch fresh basil, leaves only
    1 bunch fresh parsley, leaves only
    ½ cup (75 g) blanched garlic (see Note)
    ¾ cup (75 g) grated Parmesan cheese
    ¾ cup (100 g) pine nuts, toasted
    1 tablespoon chile flakes
    Grated zest of 1 lemon
    1 tablespoon kosher salt
    1 teaspoon freshly ground black pepper
    1¼ cups (300 ml) extra-virgin olive oil

In a food processor, combine the basil, parsley, garlic, Parmesan, pine nuts, chile flakes, lemon zest, salt, and black pepper. Pulse to combine. With the motor running, pour in the olive oil slowly and process until a smooth paste forms. Refrigerate until ready to use.

Note: To blanch the garlic, set up a bowl of ice and water. Bring a small pot of salted water to a boil. Place the whole cloves into the water and blanch for 2 minutes. Remove the garlic from the boiling water and place in the ice bath to stop the cooking and completely cool.

ORANGE CHILE OIL

MAKES 1 QUART (1 L)

A couple of years ago, I developed a chile oil with Enzo Olive Oil Company called Devil's Tears. As the name indicates, it's pretty darn intense, with a deep fire-engine red color to match. When I want something that's a little milder and more nuanced, I love making this oil at home, with a mix of chiles (whatever is in the garden or easy to get), garlic, herbs, and a little hit of orange. It will last for months, and it's great drizzled over seafood, pizza, or grilled meats.

    4 cups (960 ml) extra-virgin olive oil
    1½ ounces (40 g) mixed dried chiles (Thai bird's eye, chipotle, guajillo, árbol, etc.)
    Zest strips from 1 orange
    1 bunch fresh thyme
    3 cloves garlic, peeled

In a large pot, combine the oil, chiles, orange zest strips, thyme, and garlic and bring to a simmer over medium heat. Cook for 1 to 2 minutes to let the flavors come together. Pour the oil into an airtight container or jar and let steep for at least 8 hours before using. When you're happy with the flavor, strain the oil and store in a dark place at room temperature in a sealed container.

STEAK OIL

MAKES 3 CUPS (720 ML)

This is our go-to garnish at Miller & Lux, along with Maldon flaky sea salt. These two ingredients are all you need to beautifully finish a perfectly cooked steak. Infused with fresh herbs, garlic, peppercorns, and citrus, this has just enough going on to step it up from regular extra-virgin olive oil.

3 cups (720 ml) extra-virgin olive oil

½ bunch fresh thyme

½ bunch fresh rosemary

½ cup (75 g) garlic, smashed and peeled

1 teaspoon peppercorns

Zest strips from ½ lemon

1 bay leaf

In a medium pot, combine the oil, herbs, garlic, peppercorns, lemon zest, and bay leaf. Slowly heat, uncovered, to 250°F (120°C). Remove from the heat, cover the pot with the lid, and let cool down completely. Strain all the fried aromatics out of the oil and discard. The oil is good to use immediately, but it can be stored from 2 to 4 weeks in an airtight plastic container or glass bottle in a cool dark place, or up to 1 year in the refrigerator.

TERIYAKI SAUCE

MAKES 1½ CUPS (360 ML)

I have this super-versatile sauce with sweet and savory Asian flavors around all summer to brush onto salmon, or skewers, or to serve as a condiment for rice bowls. It does all things.

1 cup (240 ml) soy sauce

Juice of 1 lemon

1 tablespoon sake

1 tablespoon mirin

1 teaspoon rice vinegar

2 teaspoons sesame oil

½ cup (110 g) brown sugar

4 cloves garlic, grated on a Microplane

4 teaspoons grated fresh ginger

4 teaspoons sambal oelek

1 tablespoon cornstarch

In a small saucepan, combine the soy sauce, lemon juice, sake, mirin, vinegar, sesame oil, brown sugar, garlic, ginger, and sambal oelek. Bring to a simmer and cook for 2 to 3 minutes.

In a small bowl, stir together the cornstarch and ¼ cup (60 ml) water to make a slurry. Pour the slurry into the teriyaki sauce while whisking. Bring the sauce back up to a simmer and cook for another minute or two. If you notice the teriyaki sauce beginning to get too thick, you can add a little water to thin it out. Refrigerate until ready to use.

PIZZA SAUCE

MAKES 2 CUPS (480 ML)

This gets used both as the base for our red pizzas and as a dipping sauce for the open-faced grilled sausage sandwich that we call the Pork Store Special (page 70). It's incredibly simple to make and has just enough seasoning and herb flavor to make it interesting.

¼ cup (60 ml) extra-virgin olive oil

2 cloves garlic, peeled and crushed

1 can (28 ounces/794 g) tomato puree

1 can (28 ounces/794 g) crushed tomatoes

3 sprigs fresh basil

Kosher salt and freshly ground black pepper

In a large saucepan, warm the oil over medium heat until very hot but not smoking. Add the garlic, tomato puree, and crushed tomatoes. Cover and bring to a boil. Uncover, reduce the heat, and add the basil. Simmer for 30 minutes. Season to taste with salt and pepper. Store in an airtight container in the refrigerator until ready to use.

BÉCHAMEL

MAKES 4 CUPS (960 ML)

This is our other pizza sauce—one for white pizzas. A version of this is also the base for Grilled Truffle Macaroni and Cheese (page 202) and can be used for any cheese sauce.

2 tablespoons (30 g) unsalted butter

2 tablespoons all-purpose flour

1 cup (240 ml) heavy cream

1 cup (240 ml) whole milk

1 cloves garlic, minced

2 sprigs fresh thyme

1 bay leaf

Kosher salt and freshly ground black pepper

In a medium pot, melt the butter over medium heat. Add the flour to make a roux, stirring well so that it cooks evenly and turns golden blond. Whisk in the cream and milk a little bit at a time, so there are no lumps. Stir in the garlic, thyme, and bay leaf. Simmer over medium heat, stirring occasionally to prevent the bottom of the pot from scorching, until it thickens, about 10 minutes. Season the béchamel with salt and pepper. Discard the thyme stems and bay leaf.

APPLE MUSTARD

MAKES 1 CUP (240 ML)

We developed this for our Grilled Sausage Sandwiches with Giardiniera (page 106), but I liked it so much that I wanted to include it here, as a reminder that it would be a nice addition to any grilled chicken or meat. It's a hearty condiment that adds a caramelized sweetness to balance out an otherwise savory dish.

- 1 Fuji apple, diced
- ½ small yellow onion, diced
- 2 tablespoons extra-virgin olive oil
- 1 teaspoon kosher salt
- ½ teaspoon freshly ground black pepper
- 2 teaspoons whole-grain mustard
- 2 teaspoons Dijon mustard

SET UP THE GRILL

Preheat a charcoal or gas grill to medium-high heat, and set it up with two zones: a hot side and cold (less hot) side, for direct and indirect cooking. (See method, page 15.) You want the temperature to hover around 375°F (190°C).

Place the apple and onion in a bowl and drizzle with the olive oil and sprinkle with the salt and pepper. Toss until well coated. Enclose in a foil packet and place on the cooler side of the grill until everything is softened, about 30 minutes.

Transfer the apple mixture to a blender. Add both mustards and puree until smooth. Store in an airtight container in the fridge until ready to use.

AVOCADO BBQ SAUCE

MAKES 1½ TO 2 CUPS (360 TO 480 ML)

When making our Barbecue Chicken Lollipops (page 26), we came up with this fun sauce—inspired by Alabama white barbecue sauce—that gets both a green tint and a creaminess from the addition of avocado. This can serve as a sauce for grilled meat, as a dip, and also as a great sandwich spread. We've made this plenty of times since its creation and don't plan on stopping anytime soon.

- 1 avocado, halved and pitted
- ¼ bunch fresh parsley, leaves only
- ¾ cup (180 ml) mayonnaise
- ¼ cup (60 ml) sour cream
- 2 tablespoons prepared horseradish
- 1 tablespoon yellow mustard
- 1 tablespoon fresh lemon juice
- 1 teaspoon freshly ground black pepper
- ½ teaspoon kosher salt
- ½ teaspoon smoked paprika
- ¼ teaspoon garlic powder

Scoop the avocado flesh into a blender. Add all of the remaining ingredients and puree until smooth and creamy. Refrigerate until ready to use.

BORDELAISE SAUCE

MAKES 2 TO 3 CUPS (480 TO 720 ML)

We have a few signature sauces at Miller & Lux, but this one is by far our most popular. It's great with any cut of beef, adding depth and richness that comes from the layers of flavor infused into the red wine sauce. It requires very little hands-on activity but a lot of patience as it reduces into a syrupy consistency. At the restaurant we use homemade veal stock, but we're making the assumption that beef broth is an easier get for the home cook.

> ¼ cup (60 ml) extra-virgin olive oil
> ½ pound (225 g) carrots, peeled and roughly chopped
> 1 pound (455 g) shallots, peeled and roughly chopped
> ¼ pound (115 g) garlic, peeled and roughly chopped
> ¼ pound (115 g) mushrooms, cleaned and roughly chopped
> 2 teaspoons freshly ground black pepper
> ½ bunch fresh thyme
> 2 bottles (750 ml) red wine
> 4 quarts (3.8 L) beef broth
> ¼ cup (60 ml) red wine vinegar
> Kosher salt

In a large sauté pan, heat the olive oil over medium heat. Add the carrots, shallots, garlic, mushrooms, black pepper, and thyme and sauté everything, stirring occasionally, until the vegetables are tender, 5 to 6 minutes.

Add the wine to deglaze the pan and cook until reduced by three-quarters or until you have about 1 cup (240 ml) left of the wine. Add the broth and vinegar to the pan and simmer for 1 hour.

Pour the contents through a fine-mesh sieve into another tall pot. Discard all the solids. Return the liquid to medium heat and bring to a simmer. Cook until the sauce is reduced to 2 to 3 cups (480 to 720 ml), 2 to 3 hours or until or the desired consistency/thickness is reached. Season with salt to taste.

MEYER LEMON SALT

MAKES ¼ CUP (40 G)

This can be easily scaled up to make more salt. It looks nice when it comes together and stores well. A versatile seasoning, this also makes a great housewarming or host gift.

> Grated zest of 1 Meyer lemon
> ¼ cup (35 g) kosher salt
> 1 teaspoon fresh thyme leaves

Mix all of the ingredients together until well combined.

RIB AND CHICKEN DRY RUB

MAKES ABOUT 2½ CUPS (350 G)

This is without a doubt our go-to BBQ rub, with the sweet, spicy, and smoky flavors that kick up any grilled or smoked meat. All that to say, if you make only one dry rub from the book, this should be it. It makes a lot, which should last you through several meals—just keep it tightly sealed and stored in a dry place.

> 1 cup (220 g) light brown sugar
> ½ cup (55 g) smoked paprika
> ¼ cup (35 g) plus 2 tablespoons kosher salt
> 2 tablespoons onion powder
> 2 tablespoons cayenne pepper
> 2 tablespoons freshly ground black pepper
> 2 tablespoons garlic powder
> 2 tablespoons ground coriander

Mix all of the ingredients together until well combined. Store in an airtight container until ready to use.

PORCINI MUSHROOM RUB

MAKES ¾ CUP (80 G)

Porcini mushrooms add a beautiful and complex umami flavoring to food. This is what we use on our Smoked Beef Ribs Bourguignon (page 158), but I would also eat this on grilled chicken, pork, or beef, or to flavor a vegetarian main course. You can buy dried porcini mushrooms in the spice section of most grocery stores. To make the powder, add it to a spice grinder or small food processor.

- ½ cup (56 g) porcini powder
- 1½ tablespoons (13 g) kosher salt
- 1 tablespoon garlic powder
- 1 tablespoon onion powder
- 1 tablespoon freshly ground black pepper
- ½ teaspoon ground nutmeg
- 1 small bunch thyme, leaves picked

Mix all of the ingredients together until well combined. Store in an airtight container until ready to use.

BRISKET CHILE SPICE RUB

MAKES 2 CUPS (280 G)

Our signature brisket recipe gets a good coating of this dried chile rub before spending many hours in the smoker. It has heat, smokiness, and even a touch of anise flavor from the fennel. This would work well on any steak dish—I love using a little on a flank steak for tacos, and it's nice to sprinkle a bit of it on heartier shellfish like shrimp before grilling as well.

- 2 dried Anaheim chiles
- 1 ancho chile
- 2 dried chipotle chiles
- 2 tablespoons fennel seeds
- 1 tablespoon coriander seeds
- 4 to 6 black peppercorns
- ½ cup (55 g) smoked paprika
- ¼ cup (19 g) garlic powder
- ¼ cup (55 g) light brown sugar
- ½ cup (69 g) kosher salt

In a large dry skillet, toast the chiles, fennel seeds, coriander seeds, and peppercorns over medium-high heat until fragrant, about 2 minutes. Add to a spice grinder and run until you have a fine powder. In a large bowl, combine the spices with the smoked paprika, garlic powder, brown sugar, and salt. Store in an airtight container until ready to use.

ACKNOWLEDGMENTS

IF YOU'RE LUCKY, YOU SOMETIMES FIND YOURSELF AT A POINT IN LIFE WHEN IT FEELS LIKE YOU'RE EXACTLY WHERE YOU'RE MEANT TO BE. I've worked in, and launched, many restaurants in my career. But it wasn't until I partnered with Joe Lacob, Peter Guber, and the Golden State Warriors to open the doors at Miller & Lux, my modern American steakhouse in San Francisco, that I felt like I had found home. This classic American steak concept is the brand I have dreamt of since I was a child, and it so naturally translates to the type of cooking and entertaining I do at home. This book is such a reflection of this phase of my life, and I couldn't be more grateful for it.

Of course, these things never happen in a vacuum, and I wouldn't be here without the tremendous support of my people, both at work and at home.

A huge shout-out to Andy O'Day and our hardworking teams at Miller & Lux, Wayfare Tavern, Miller & Lux Hualalai, Miller & Lux Provisions, Town Hall, and future restaurants from The Greater Organization. It's an absolute pleasure to work with all of you every day.

This book was meticulously handcrafted by the dedicated team at my production company, Monarch Collective, which has been responsible for all our print and digital media and television production over much of the last decade. Thank you for making my dreams a reality in this book and beyond: Amanda Gold, my creative partner; Matt Masera, my culinary partner; Donna Perreault, my tireless chief of staff, and the rest of the crew who helped bring these pages to life—photographer Jason Perry and recipe testers and stylists Anna Voloshyna and Eric Lundy. Thank you, too, to my agent, Michael Psaltis, who has seen me through so many of my book projects.

We've absolutely loved this first collaboration with Abrams—thank you to Holly Dolce, Juliet Dore, Danielle Youngsmith, and the rest of the team for understanding my vision and turning it into something incredible. Here's to many more.

Last but not least, big love to the family—Tolan, Miles, Hayden, Dorothy, Leroy, Frank, Floyd, and Mazzy the Pig.

INDEX

Editors: Holly Dolce and Juliet Dore
Designer: Danielle Youngsmith
Managing Editors: Glenn Ramirez and Lisa Silverman
Production Managers: Kathleen Gaffney and
    Sarah Masterson Hally

Library of Congress Control Number:
2023949055

ISBN: 978-1-4197-6995-5
Exclusive Edition: 978-1-4197-7530-7
eISBN: 979-8-88707-105-3

Text copyright © 2024 Tyler Florence
Photographs copyright © 2024 Jason Perry,
except pp. 18, 162, and 163 by Matt Masera
and pp. 141 and 251 by Zach Burghardt

Cover © 2024 Abrams

Published in 2024 by Abrams, an imprint of ABRAMS. All rights reserved.
No portion of this book may be reproduced, stored in a retrieval system, or
transmitted in any form or by any means, mechanical, electronic, photocopy-
ing, recording, or otherwise, without written permission from the publisher.

Printed and bound in China
10 9 8 7 6 5 4 3 2 1

Abrams books are available at special discounts when purchased in quantity
for premiums and promotions as well as fundraising or educational use.
Special editions can also be created to specification. For details, contact
specialsales@abramsbooks.com or the address below.

Abrams® is a registered trademark of Harry N. Abrams, Inc.

ABRAMS The Art of Books
195 Broadway, New York, NY 10007
abramsbooks.com